WIRRAL

THE GOLDEN YEARS

The publishers would like to thank the following companies for their support in the production of this book

Main Sponsor

Technical Demolition Services Ltd

Abbeyfield Hoylake & West Kirby Society

Bromborough Paints Ltd

Carmet Tug Co. Ltd

Cereal Partners UK

James Cubbin & Son

Gordale Nurseries Ltd

Grantreel Construction Ltd

Lees Solicitors LLP

Mostyn House School

W.E. Parsons & Co. Ltd

Quinns of Greasby

First published in Great Britain by True North Books Limited
England HX3 6SN
01422 244555

ISBN 978 - 1906649272

Text, design and origination by True North Books

Introduction from Tony Taperell

On behalf of Technical Demolition Services I would like to take this opportunity to welcome you to this fantastic book 'Wirral - The Golden Years', which we are delighted to be featured in.

We are proud to become a piece of Wirral's rich historical reading, and to tell you the story of a local company rising to become a world leader in our specialist field.

'Wirral - The Golden Years' offers you the chance of recapturing the spirit of a bygone era, fondly remembering a mis-spent youth, or reminiscing, perhaps only fleetingly, about memories from times past. For some of you this book may provide an insight in to life before you were born.

We at Technical Demolition Services will always be filled with a sense of respect for the past. Understanding the nostalgia associated with the architectural heritage and craftsmanship of previous generations forming a vibrant tapestry to be read and interpreted by our demolition expertise.

The demolition of any building or structure brings us directly in to contact with the heritage and human interest stories that have formed, been associated with and accumulated during the structure's lifespan. Histories sometimes passed from generation to generation.

But, although it is to sad to see the end of once magnificent structures, we at Technical Demolition Services feel immense pride that we are enabling renewal and regeneration, new opportunities in providing fresh and new hopes for new generations.

We hope that in reading this book you will join us in our view that an appreciation of our heritage illuminates our vision to look forward to the future.

Starting from a father and son business, and evolving to our current status enjoying demolition world leadership. We are proud that Technical Demolition Services are pioneering projects, innovatively inspiring new methods of working, utilising the strength of our mighty fleet of demolition machinery and energising the demolition world, constantly striving forwards for others to watch and attempt to follow.

We are proud to have our business now firmly established in Wirral, offering expertise that our competitors find impossible to follow, and we are proud to refer to the area as home. We hope that you will enjoy reading about the nostalgia of our journey as a company as much as we have enjoyed the opportunity to reminisce!

Tony G. Taperell
Chairman and Managing Director

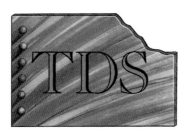

CONTENTS

BEYOND LIVING MEMORY: the beginning of a century
PAGE 6

BACK TO OUR ROOTS: rural life
PAGE 12

BUILDING FOR A NEW WORLD: from river to big pond
PAGE 20

LOOKING DOWN: the bigger picture
PAGE 30

DAYS TO REMEMBER: with joy and sadness
PAGE 50

STREET WISE: a change of view
PAGE 60

NOW THEN!: pause for reflection
PAGE 78

HAVE WHEELS, WILL TRAVEL: moving on
PAGE 86

SHOP-PORTUNITIES!: retail therapy
PAGE 96

FUN AND GAMES: relax and enjoy
PAGE 100

A HARD DAY'S GRAFT: working life
PAGE 114

INTRODUCTION

We welcome you to a gentle meander through the last 100 years, illustrating in words and pictures the changing patterns of daily life. The pace of life, today, can often leave us breathless and trailing in its wake. Having attempted, recently, to explain to my god-daughters, aged 12 and 15, what life was like without computers, I am more than aware of the life-changing inventions that have re-shaped our lives!

100 years ago, before the car, it was horse, bicycle or your own two feet, followed, later, by public transport; yet, how many of us today turn our nose up at using public transport? In 1900, many people lived their lives within a mile of their front door: rail travel, from the mid-19th century, was a revelation but did not address, at first, the need to get to smaller places and had limited impact. Travel and knowledge of other cultures was limited to the well-off and such experiences were straight out of adventure books for boys and girls!

Life for our ancestors was often harder but their lives were simpler with fewer choices to make. Expressions that we wrestle with on a regular basis today, such as work/life balance, career change, mature student, re-training were not part of their vocabulary and recent technology has played a massive part in changing our day to day experiences.

Surrounded as it was, and is, by water, sandwiched between the Dee and the Mersey and crowned by the Irish Sea, the Wirral was a quiet backwater, content with its self-sustaining and small scale farming and fishing. In the early twelfth century, a priory was founded in Birkenhead, so-called after indigenous local birch trees. One hundred and eighty years later, the monks established a ferry service for public use across the Mersey, around which a settlement established itself around the priory. When the Industrial Revolution stirred the country into feverish and sustained activity, life in the Wirral changed radically in a short space of time. With the introduction of the new steam-powered ferries, the more affluent merchants from Liverpool saw the Wirral as an ideal site for their large and palatial residences and estates, which in turn triggered the establishment of small-scale businesses to service their needs. As a result of the intense shipping activity across the Mersey, in and around Liverpool, industrial activity on the Wirral side of the river was gathering pace by 1850. Mr. Laird (of the later and famous Cammell Laird shipyards), the Lever Brothers, with their soap and detergent factories and many other notable businessmen of the day, transformed the look of the west bank of the Mersey and provided myriad new opportunities for workers in the region. Small settlements grew and prospered in this Victorian flurry of activity. Thankfully, pockets of quiet and diverse unspoilt landscape remained intact to remind us all of the Wirral's unique character and attraction.

We take pleasure in including in this book, histories of an outstanding selection of companies and organisations, which have contributed to the sustainability of the region's economic achievements. With their co-operation and access to their archives, we have been able to tell their stories and, hopefully, this will revive the memories of those who have worked for them or been touched by their part in community life.

For all of us, memories are the currency which we use to record the changes and progress in our everyday lives and our place as individuals in the greater scheme of things. Whether our memories are joyful or sad, they are the 'filling' which creates the sandwich of our lives. Meandering through a pictorial cross-section of life in the Wirral will inevitably remind us of the experience of our own lives. We hope this generic and random glimpse of the Wirral will trigger smiles and laughter as you make this journey with your family, friends and colleagues – enjoy!

TEXT	DEREK GREENWOOD
PHOTOGRAPH COMPILATION	DEREK GREENWOOD
DESIGNER	SEAMUS MOLLOY
BUSINESS DEVELOPMENT EDITOR	PETER PREST

BEYOND LIVING MEMORY
The beginning of a century

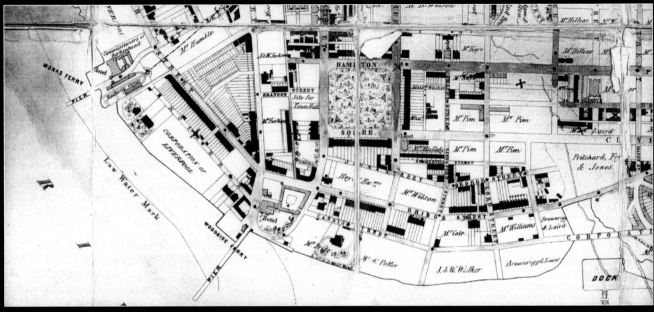

During the nineteenth century, from the beginnings of the Industrial Revolution in the 1830s, the Wirral Peninsular took on a changing and chameleon-like role, adapting, in places, to new industrial activity and thriving on its position across the River Mersey from Liverpool. Elsewhere, the landscape evolved more slowly, establishing for itself a role, initially, as a rural dormitory for the wealthy industrialists of Liverpool. As industries expanded through the nineteenth century on the eastern fringe of the peninsular, the demand for a substantially expanding workforce created a need for homes, shops and other businesses to serve the working people of the area. The establishment of a steam-powered ferry service across the Mersey enticed and attracted new visitors and residents to 'the other side'. The Wirral became fashionable on both its coasts and struggled to keep up to the demand for anything and everything, from jobs and housing, to beaches and traditional seaside attractions for visitors. For the residents of Liverpool it was a readily accessible day trip to the seaside. Through the latter part of the nineteenth century and the early part of the twentieth century, travel and transport changed radically. Railways, from the 1840s had made travel to 'far-away' places possible, at first only for the well-off. By the beginning of the twentieth century railway travel had become more accessible to many more people and widespread local bus travel was only twenty years away. Mass movement of people on a daily basis was to initiate massive innovation in living and working as everybody's personal world was enlarged.

Above: As in many other towns throughout Britain, the first forty years of the nineteenth century provided an opportunity

for seismic change. The rapid development of places in possession of useable natural resources or a fortuitous position in the topography of a region, created a magnet for new industry

on a scale which demanded the movement of workers from one part of the country to another. Having established on its west and east coast a hundred years earlier, a shipping industry in all its forms, the Wirral Peninsular was handily placed to take advantage of this sudden surge of industrial activity. Unfortunately, shipping along the west coast, including the regular service of packet boats to Ireland, had virtually ceased by 1820, the natural tendency of the River Dee to silt up preventing anything other than small-scale pleasure shipping on the west coast of the peninsular. The east coast, however, offered more exciting large-scale opportunities for every aspect of shipping. This section of a plan of Birkenhead, created by John Law in 1845, already hints at the development of a civic pattern to the layout of new private and public developments within the town. With successful industry came wealth, influence, prestige and status and the civic leaders demanded that this was a visible and improving impression of the town as promoted to the rest of the country and the rest of the world.

Below: This 1920 picture of the pier at New Brighton, opened in 1867, shows a traditional British Victorian pier. Strangely empty of people, this view was probably taken early on a Sunday morning. It replaced a previous structure which existed purely to receive and despatch ferries across the river and was acquired by the local council at the end of the 1920s, restored and re-opened in 1931. The town was developed in the early nineteenth century by a Liverpool merchant, James Atherton, who purchased land around Rock Point with the specific intention of creating a desirable and elegant resort and residential area for the better off, not dissimilar to Brighton on the Sussex coast. Fifty years later, New Brighton had established itself as a regular holiday destination for the populations of many Lancashire industrial towns as well as for Liverpool. The town's popularity was boosted at the end of the century by the construction of the New Brighton Tower between 1897 and 1900. Higher than Blackpool Tower at 562 feet, its presence was short-lived due to inadequate maintenance during World War I. It was demolished between 1919 and 1921 for safety reasons. New Brighton held its popularity throughout World War II and its pier and funfair played a part in helping families to put aside for a few short hours their worries and worst fears about members of their family slugging it out on some European front with the enemy. Their own safety was also under threat because of the obvious target the area presented as a major provider of ships. The nights were often dangerous as the Luftwaffe filled the sky with their squadrons attacking the shipyards and those who worked around the clock to build and maintain the fighting ships required in such a conflict. Not a time to be romantically wandering along the exposed promenade! The end of hostilities in 1945 saw a steady decline in the town's fortunes, an increase in personal wealth after the austerity of wartime generally sending holidaymakers further afield. The affluence and fashions of the 1960s kept New Brighton going, but by the end of the decade its heyday was over and at the end of the 1972 season the pier closed, to be demolished six years later.

beyond their years. Take the boy, second from the right on the back row, and the girl, in the centre of the middle row, and we see faces and expressions that might fit a forty or fifty-year-old. The sadness and weariness of poverty invades every expression here. Even those still able to empty their heads for a moment, such as the girl on the far right of the middle row, reveal the impossibility of hope or a future with progress. Beyond the reluctance and curiosity for the newness of the camera, some, such as the boys second left and far right on the back row, the girl and boy far left and second left on the middle row, and the boys first left and centre on the front row, show simple fear and uncertainty for a world which they are struggling to be part of. For a hundred years since this picture was taken, how many times have we all witnessed similar images of poverty of life, education and experience?

Above: A mass influx of poorer, working people to any area creates a sudden demand for housing and services. After seventy years of industrial endeavour, it might be expected that a means of supporting the needs of these people could and would have been a priority, if not for reasons of philanthropy then for reasons of security in terms of continuous output. Organisations, faiths and, occasionally companies, set up hostels or missions to provide the basic needs absent from the lives of those struggling to find their role in a profoundly changed society. By the turn of the twentieth century, these needs were magnified as a result of massive increases in the demand for workers on particular sites near to the centres of towns and cities. This picture of 'Mission Children', taken in Birkenhead around 1900, presents us with a dramatic and visual range of emotions. Firstly, we note that, despite all the children pictured here probably being under the age of 10, their faces reveal a lifetime of hardship and experience far

Below: The small town of Bebington, situated just south of Birkenhead, can trace its roots back to Saxon times, whilst its church supports a history of a community in the area from the 14th century. The opening of a railway station in the town in the 1830s and the consequent influx of new workers to the area was the

main spur to the enlargement of the community. Getting a 'decent education' has always been the wish of our parents. Pressure to achieve more than they achieved in their school years has been felt by most of us. In 1900, education was straight forward and the same across the country and, as today, the priorities of reading and writing were to the fore, seen as the key to all other aspects of learning. Bebington School, where this photograph of Group 1 and their teacher was taken in 1898, gave students the 'luxury' of some freedom in terms of their school outfits, long or three-quarter length trousers, for example. Interesting to note that the teacher looks little different to masters we recall sixty years later at a boys only grammar school.

Above: This picture, taken in the Back Chester Street area of Birkenhead around 1910, shows us residential street life in an industrial town. A hint of sunshine, and mothers were tempted into the street with their children. Their accommodation was basic and dark, with little, if any, light or heat. Streets were largely traffic-free and putting the pram on the edge of the road rather than the pavement proved relatively safe. Motorised traffic had barely been introduced and any vehicles were hand or horse-drawn. Passing the time of day was a welcome intrusion into their lives.

Above: A night out at the Theatre Royal, Birkenhead, in 1909, when this photograph was taken, probably required a journey in a horse and carriage, unless you lived within walking distance. Motor-powered buses had arrived but were in their infancy with all the limitations which that implied, limited service, limited routes, etc. Before World War I, provincial theatre was often about music hall, a light-hearted miscellany of performances to warm the heart and to fill the evening and put a smile on everybody's face. Silent films were providing some competition although nothing could compare with a live performance. Until television became an option in at least every other home fifty years later, a night out at the theatre or at the cinema was often the weekly treat for many, a chance to get out of the house, dress up in a best frock and meet up with friends. It is hard for us to imagine today, a world of entertainment 'on tap', so to speak, without the omnipresent television. Provincial repertory theatres, with small companies performing classic staples of popular drama, were often responsible for providing this opportunity.

Right: This delightful and idyllic view of the beach and promenade at Egremont, taken at the turn of the twentieth century, belies the reality of a busy industrialised waterfront on this and the opposite side of the River Mersey. A businessman, Captain John Askew, who saw the development of Merseyside as a great opportunity for his own ideas, built a substantial house as his home in the area, in 1835, and named the house 'Egremont' after his birthplace in Cumberland. Sometime later, the town that developed here took its name from the house. By this time, this north-east corner of the Wirral peninsular had already successfully cultivated an identity as a refined and worthwhile 'spot' for visitors to enjoy a traditional day out at the seaside. In the centre background of the picture can be seen the New Brighton Tower. At one time, the pier at Egremont was the longest on Merseyside. However, after being hit by a drifting oil tanker in 1932 and in 1941 by a coaster, Wallasey Corporation decided, on the grounds of cost alone, that it would be better to take it down. This they did in 1946.

BACK TO OUR ROOTS
Rural life

Whilst areas adjacent to the east coast of the Wirral Peninsular had already begun to embrace technology and industry in the latter part of the nineteenth century, the introduction of the railways to the Wirral enabled access to markets elsewhere by land as well as by sea and also opened up the region to visitors from further afield. The settling of the wealthier classes in the mid-eighteenth century certainly brought a degree of gentility to the Wirral and saw the development of smaller settlements in the more rural areas.

Below: Bidtson Hill, an area of natural and tranquil heath and woodland, in denial of its position amidst the endless urban busy-ness of Birkenhead and its suburbs, promotes on its upper slopes, in the shape of two large and prominent white domes, the Bidston Observatory. It was built in 1866, using predominantly local sandstone, on part of an estate belonging to Lord Vyner, a local landowner and businessman. A philanthropic gesture enabled a deal to be done, at the turn of the twentieth century, to place Bidston Hill into local authority ownership, on a conditional requirement that the area would 'remain an open space for public recreation and maintained in a wild and natural state'. The Observatory originally housed

equatorial and transit telescopes in its two white domes and, at the beginning of the twentieth century, also housed pioneering equipment designed to measure seismic activity. The late 1920s saw the arrival in the Observatory of the Liverpool Tidal Institute, analysing and predicting tides. The Institute was amalgamated under the direction of the director, Joseph Proudman, and during World War II, predicted tides ahead of the D-Day Landings. In 1962, the telescopes at the Observatory were removed and the historic artefacts placed in the collection of the Liverpool Museum. For many years, at one o'clock each day, a gun was fired in Birkenhead Dock to mark the exact time for the benefit of residents and workers in the Wirral and in Liverpool, triggered by a telegraphic line from the Observatory. The gun was fired for a final time on July 18, 1969, the same year in which the Proudman Oceanographic Laboratory became an independent institute. In 1975, the Observatory at Bidston became home to the British Oceanographic Data Centre, originally set up in 1969, which became part of the Institute of Oceanographic Sciences. After the Oceanographic Laboratory was transferred to the campus of Liverpool University in 2004-5, the Observatory, sadly, became unused.

Above: Outside the main urban areas of the peninsular, the Wirral consists of a gentle rural hinterland, un-dramatic but with many trees. Until 1830, this hinterland was almost totally unsullied, as industry had not yet impacted outside the docks area of Birkenhead and Wallasey. As the century progressed and industrial activity on both sides of the Mersey brought new people into the region, both to live and work, the attraction of the peninsular's 'green pastures' saw substantial residential development from east to west, enlarging communities and extending essential support services across the region. By the turn of the twentieth century, the quiet serenity of the Wirral had ebbed away in some places to be replaced by new housing for the increased volume of 'in-comers'. Well-established resorts such as Hoylake and New Brighton also expanded, serving residents and visitors alike. The Mersey railway tunnel, opening in 1886, had spawned a network of rail links across the Wirral which, by the early 1920s, made it relatively easy to commute into Liverpool. By 1952, when this picture was taken, pockets of housing had sprung up across the peninsular to satisfy the need for housing workers arriving to service the post-war boom. Searching for the forgotten corners, the under-populated areas, the rural gems of architecture and un-sullied areas of natural beauty in the Wirral Peninsular is now much harder to successfully achieve – but is still possible, with some patience.

Right: The windmill at Bidston, seen here mid-twentieth century, was built around the turn of the nineteenth century on top of Bidston Hill and operated as a fully functional mill, grinding corn to flour, until the end of the 1870s, from whence it fell into an increasing state of disrepair. Interestingly, the top of the windmill could be turned through 360 degrees to enable the best advantage to be retrieved from the prevailing wind direction. Originally restored in 1894, the building, sails and machinery were finally restored in the 1990s to the benefit of visitors to the area.

Below: Mentioned in the Domesday Book as Bernestone, Barnston is now home to around 3,500

residents. It lies in a rural position north east of Heswall. This winter view of the village of Barnston, probably taken in the mid-twentieth century, typifies the semi-rural nature of much of the Peninsular, with mass housing development generally concentrated on the fringes of the larger communities within easy reach of work opportunities. Barnston's most memorable night over the last fifty years was on March 24, 1962, when a small Merseyside group donned suits for the first time and filled Barnston's Women's Institute for the first sell-out gig of their careers. It was, of course, The Beatles.

Right: The town of West Kirby originated as a Viking settlement – the name Kirby meaning 'a village with a church'. The town has gravitated from its original site around the church to expand adjacent to the railway station with a line which extends across the Peninsular, under the Mersey and into the centre of Liverpool. This rural, traffic-free scene of Nook Farm and the Ring of Bells in the old village of West Kirby, taken in the early twentieth century, epitomises the village 'quiet life' for which the Peninsular was previously so well known.

Below: For the first decades of the twentieth century, as this photograph of rural Wirral shows, much farm machinery was mechanical and un-motorised and would be repaired by the farmer himself or by the village blacksmith. The fettling of metal was an integral part of farming life. Horse-power was the only power, however vast the field, as in this view, or however steep the gradient. Harvest time was extremely labour intensive requiring the services of every horse, man, woman and child.

From the Middle Ages and through the eighteenth century, the Anglo-Saxon settlement of Eastham was a well-established and well-used ferry crossing point to and from Liverpool. Business declined in the middle of the nineteenth century with the spread of the rail network, including a direct line from Chester to Woodside Ferry in Birkenhead, providing a shorter and more direct ferry crossing. In 1846, the ferry owner and operator, Thomas Stanley, constructed the Eastham Ferry Hotel, followed by the Pleasure Gardens, substantial floral and landscaped gardens with all the usual Victorian delights such as a bandstand, boating lake, open-air stage and, would you believe it, a zoo. The zoo collection included lions, monkeys, bears and other wildlife and the Pleasure Gardens successfully lured in a new and regular clientele. In 1897, a Jubilee Arch was built at the entrance to the Gardens to commemorate Queen Victoria's Diamond Jubilee. Three years earlier, the Manchester Ship Canal had opened, bringing in new business and enabling relatively substantial ships to sail inland as far as Salford and Manchester. The Eastham Ferry Hotel, seen here at the height of its popularity in 1920, was enjoying its position at the Chester end of the Peninsular, in the shadow of the seaward end of the Manchester Ship Canal and its accompanying docks and Eastham Lock. The Stanlow Oil Refinery had also opened, east of the nearby burgeoning industrial dockland at Ellesmere Port. The potential for a thriving, well-presented luxury hotel was endless and its relative proximity to Chester and Liverpool added to its success. The high density of people seen here at the front of the hotel suggests a high-profile visitor or, perhaps, a major sporting event. By the late 1920s, the area began to decline; the ferry closed and the Gardens fell into disrepair during the 1930s. Only forty years later, during European Conservation Year, were the former Gardens designated a Woodland and Country Park and returned to local people and visitors as a relaxing and popular area for recreation.

Above and right: Hard as it might be to believe now, at the turn of the eighteenth century, the small town of Parkgate, on the west coast of the peninsular, enjoyed a deep-water anchorage in the River Dee estuary. The River Dee was a shipping lane for the city of Chester, but silting up had necessitated the establishment of a suitable port further upstream and a quay and anchorage was originally built at Neston. However, this, also silted up and a quay was built at Parkgate, near the gate of Neston's hunting park, and this became the main terminal for packet boats carrying mail between England and Dublin. These passenger—carrying boats also took some of the great literary and cultural figures of the day across the Irish Sea, such as the composer Handel, Jonathan Swift, the author of 'Gulliver's Travels', and the notable religious leader John Wesley. Parkgate had already established itself as a fashion-

able holiday resort, with its spectacular views across the Dee estuary to North Wales. It was also well-known for the apparent curative properties of the Dee estuary mud, so well-known that Lord Nelson's mistress, Lady Emma Hamilton, born in nearby Ness, was tempted to try it out! Nelson and his mistress stayed in a local hostelry, as did Georg Friedrich Handel in April 1742, on his way to Dublin for the first performance of his 'Messiah', which he had completed in the previous summer. It was the mud that slowly, but surely, radically changed the view from the Parkgate Parade. This had an impact on the movements of boats in the estuary and, by 1810, the route to Dublin had virtually ceased operation; the only marine activity to flourish off Parkgate was shrimp fishing. In this photograph, taken at the turn of the century, looking to the right we witness a 'sea of mud'. It did not, however, stop families recognising it as an 'easy to get to' village by the sea. Almost fifty years later, some will remember the happy scoffing of shrimps and ice-cream at the Boathouse Tea Rooms. By the 1930s, the sea was still just

about reaching the sea wall at every high tide, although this picture taken on a very stormy day ten years later, in 1940, was a dramatic exception. At the end of World War II, Parkgate flourished as a desirable residential area. Views of the sea from the Parade at Parkgate have, however, been scarce, with salt marsh being the predominant feature of the immediate foreground.

Below: Many residents of, and visitors to, the Wirral might wish this idyllic image of the Peninsular was still a typical representation of daily life in the region. Sadly, this is not so, but perhaps we can be reminded to search out the quiet and natural corners of the landscape which do still exist if we search the 'interior'. This photograph, taken in 1944, has the advantage of wartime emptiness, little traffic and the slower pace of simple, rural values epitomised by the cart being pushed by hand. Remove the Morris 8 hurtling slowly towards us from the middle ground and it really *could* be a Constable from almost two centuries before.

BUILDING FOR A NEW WORLD

From river to big pond

The mouth of a river, any river, offers the opportunity to sail ships into and across the nearby ocean: but first you must build the ships. In 1330, the Benedictine monks of 'Birchen Head' Priory received the rights from King Edward II to ferry travellers from Monk's Ferry to the other side of the River Mersey. After the dissolution of the Priory in 1536 by Henry VIII, ferry rights were transferred to the wealthy landowners of the area. The boats at this time were, of course, sail-powered and the prevailing tides and cross-winds ensured a somewhat dramatic, dangerous and intermittent service across the river until the advent of steam-powered vessels at the beginning of the nineteenth century. A hundred years later, the Seacombe Ferry was transporting over 30 million passengers per year. The reign of Queen Victoria and the advent of the Industrial Revolution saw the creation of a worldwide empire, for better or worse, which depended on the ability of British industry to design and build the vessels which took our more adventurous explorers and traders to the other side of the world. From 1810 to 1850, a small hamlet lying on the east coast of the peninsular, opposite Liverpool, saw unprecedented development as its Mersey waterfront and Wallasey Creek were converted into a huge and impressive shipbuilding operation.

The Docks, Ellesmere Port

Pioneers in the construction of iron ships were John Laird and his son William, whose boiler works and shipyard was established in 1824. Their influence on Birkenhead was all-embracing as he also planned the town's layout on a grid plan. Laird's business was combined, in 1903, with Cammell's successful shipbuilding company and continued to occupy an important position as a major employer in the town for almost another century.

The River Mersey witnessed the mass emigration of families from Central and Eastern Europe to the so-called 'New World', now better known as the United States of America. Who hasn't wondered where all those 'Americans', with strange and wonderful names which appear on the credits at the end of almost every film, came from? We do know that tens of thousands of Europeans sailed out of the Mersey to a new and, sometimes, better life across the 'big pond'.

Left: At the turn of the twentieth century, the influence on trade and services of engine-powered shipping was taken for granted. Whilst some smaller enterprises hung onto the notion of sail-powered shipping, often through reasons of cost, the revolution had arrived and progressed the movement of goods and people around the world to a new and speedier level. Ellesmere Port originated as a port at the end of the Ellesmere Canal, constructed from Ellesmere in Shropshire by William Jessop and Thomas Telford with the intention to provide a route connecting the rivers

Severn, Dee and Mersey. The canal joined the River Mersey at the village of Netherpool, which later became known as the Port of Ellesmere which in turn, in the early nineteenth century became Ellesmere Port. Life in the town centred around shipping activity, the first main street taking the name of Dock Street. The involvement of the eminent industrial engineer, Thomas Telford, ensured that Ellesmere Port had a complete and beautifully designed dockland with locks, docks and warehouses. After Telford's death in 1834, his unfinished designs and ideas for the dockland were completed sympathetically by the well-known builder, Thomas Cubbit. With the development of the Manchester Ship Canal, opened in 1894, and the opening of the Stanlow Oil Terminal in the mid 1920s, the prosperity of the town and its docks was assured. Whilst industrial activity had prospered through the twentieth century, by the 1990s it had declined and people moved to Ellesmere Port for other reasons. Although the Vauxhall car plant is, for now, still one of the biggest employers in the area, other industrial ventures have been less fortunate. This view of the docks at Ellesmere Port was probably taken just before the turn of the twentieth century with sail still much in evidence.

Above: This view of the 'Thistle', a ferry on the River Mersey, was taken around 1900. At this time ferries like the 'Thistle', built in 1891 and plying between Liverpool and Wallasey, were paddle steamers.

The extremely short life in service of this great ship, together with its controversial and ignominious sinking off the southern coast of Ireland in May 1915, have presented a long-standing and controversial enigma for historians across the world over the last ninety years.

The S.S. Lusitania was commissioned by the Cunard Line and construction began at the John Brown Clydebank Yard in 1904, with a launch two years later. After teething problems during her sea trials, the ship eventually left Liverpool on September 7, 1907 on her maiden voyage to New York, arriving six days later. The Lusitania and her sister ship, Mauretania, plied the North Atlantic until the onset of war in 1914.

This picture of the S.S. Lusitania on the River Mersey was probably taken around 1912. The approach of conflict persuaded the Admiralty to make important decisions regarding the larger merchant and passenger ships. In 1914, the Lusitania was listed as an Armed Merchant Cruiser although the government had decided not to use her in this role as she was less than economical on fuel. Alongside the newer ship, Aquitania, she continued to ply the North Atlantic route primarily as a passenger ship. At the beginning of 1915, the German government declared all the seas around the British Isles a war zone. Awaiting a return journey from New York on May 1st 1915, the Lusitania had been subject to extreme warnings from the German Embassy in Washington.

The ship sailed with almost 2,000 people on board, with Fastnet Rock off the southern coast of Ireland the designated landfall. As the vessel approached the area, the captain was informed by radio of German submarine activities in the area, and decided, at this point, to change course to a north-easterly route which he believed would be safer. In enveloping fog, 30 miles off the coast, en route to the port of Queenstown, German submarine U-20 fired its one remaining torpedo towards the Lusitania, hitting it below the bridge on the starboard side. It took a mere 18 minutes and 8 miles for the ship to sink. After the explosion the engines were on full throttle with no means of closing them down hence the substantial distance covered as the ship slowly sank, with the loss of 1,195 lives.

Much of the reaction in Germany was hostile towards the sinking of the ship and the ensuing arguments in America, Britain and Germany complicated government response to the event. The controversy over the rules of conflict at the time, the observance or not of these rules by each country, the details of ambiguous cargo allegedly being carried on the ship, evidence of alleged later Royal Navy intervention at the site of the Lusitania and its impact on wreck analysis, all served to cloud the true detail of this event and its aftermath.

In its short nine years of service, this great vessel continues, sadly, to be best known for the circumstances of its demise.

Above: This view of the Mersey estuary was taken in 1936 and barely hints at the industrial nature of some parts of the Peninsular.

Right: The first 'Mauretania', nicknamed 'the Grand Old Lady', was launched in 1906 from the Swan Hunter and Wigham Richardson shipyard at Wallsend on the River Tyne. With steam turbine propulsion, she was, at the time, the largest and fastest ship in the world, noted for her luxury and speed. Within a month of her launch, the 'Mauretania' had captured the coveted Blue Riband for the fastest eastbound crossing of the Atlantic and, two years later, captured the record for the westbound crossing. After service as a troop and hospital ship during the First World War, the 'Mauretania' returned to Atlantic duties until 1930, when she became a cruise line until being withdrawn from service having made 269 double journeys across the 'big pond'.

The expertise of the Mersey shipyards was world renowned when the Cunard Shipping Company began the search for a company to build a 'new Mauretania' for its White Star Line. The Cammell Laird Yard was chosen to build the new ship, which was to be smaller than its predecessor and classed as an intermediate North Atlantic liner. Cammell Laird had built some of the largest vessels afloat at the turn of the twentieth century and, in 1920, had built the first ever all-welded ship.

This photograph shows the 'Mauretania' sliding down the slipway at the Cammell Laird yard into the peaceful waters of the River Mersey on July 28, 1938. Less than two years later, this 35,739 ton liner had been converted into a troop carrier and thrust into the dark and threatening waters of World War II. In 1946, she returned to passenger service and was refitted in 1957 and 1962, before being retired, after a final voyage to New York and a cruise in the Mediterranean, in 1965. The 'Mauretania' was the largest liner built on the Mersey until the launch of the 'Windsor Castle' in 1959.

The slipping into receivership of Cammell Laird in 2001 brought the docks to the end of an era. Fortunately, for the local skilled workers, the yard was sold and the new owners, specialising in ship repair and conversion, eventually, after a seven year wait, bought the right to use the Cammell Laird name.

Right: John Laird laid the foundations of his family's shipbuilding business in Birkenhead in the 1820s, a business further developed by his son William and the family exercised considerable influence, both financial and architectural, on the laying out of a grand design for the town centre of Birkenhead with the help of the architect James Gillespie Graham. Graham's designs, with the encouragement of the Lairds, gave a nod of acknowledgement to the 'new town' of Edinburgh and provided a grand and solid backdrop to the functional and heavily industrial landscape of the riverside. Without first-hand experience of the docks it is, perhaps, difficult to appreciate the massive scale and bulk of shipbuilding in all its variety. This photograph, taken in the Cammell Laird yard in 1948, at least gives an impression of the disproportionate scale of construction, even compared with the creation of large public buildings. Given Jonathan Swift's connection with the west coast of the Wirral, perhaps it is merely an extravagant coincidence that provided the east coast with a 'giants' landscape' on the riverside at Birkenhead. The hugeness of this industry was always a part of the Cammell Laird story. Just look at the massive and dangerous size of the links in the chains

in the foreground of this picture. The largest floating dock in the world was built at Birkenhead in 1912, and until the ' Windsor Castle' was launched in 1959, the second ship to be named 'Mauretania' was the largest liner to be built on Merseyside. Years later, after the yard had become part of British Shipbuilders, a huge construction hall was built in 1978 for 'indoor' shipbuilding.

Left: A ferry service began from Seacombe way back in the middle of the seventeenth century, and in Victorian times it was only one of ten embarkation points for crossing the River Mersey. By the 1920s, 32 million people were being carried each year on the ten minute journey. In the mid 1800s, Seacombe had become a busy shipbuilding centre, but its ferry and terminal are its main claim to fame, thanks in part, to a certain Mr. Marsden and his Pacemakers, who recorded 'Ferry Across the Mersey' in 1964 and saw it rocket up the pop music charts of the day. This still iconic and enduring song, which has become an anthem for Merseysiders, was, apparently, inspired by the Seacombe ferry and terminal, seen here in 1952.

Below: For nearly five hundred years there has been intensive marine activity on the River Mersey waterfront at Woodside, almost directly opposite to the iconic Royal Liver Building on the Liverpool side of the river. A stone pier and a small lighthouse were built around 1850, followed by a floating landing stage in the 1860s, offering better facilities for the ferries operating across the river. These facilities were improved again at the turn of the century as the paddle steamers were retired and new twin screw steamers were introduced. Inevitably, the dominance of the ferries was curbed by the Mersey railway tunnel, built in 1886. The building of the Queensway Road Tunnel in 1934 was yet another 'kick in the teeth' for the ferry operators. By the 1990s, Woodside had lost its relevance as a major interchange for different forms of transport. Agreeably, despite the demolition of the original terminal building, restoration of other aspects of the terminal have taken place in recent times to form a tourist opportunity of interest to both locals and visitors. This picture of Woodside Terminal, taken in 1954, is almost the perfect view across the river, with the 'Reina del Pacifico' liner providing an impressive backdrop to the terminal, with the Royal Liver Building, the Cunard Steamship Company Building and the dome of the Mersey Docks and Harbour Board. Double-decker buses of the period are much in evidence, still at this time with their open platforms at the back, demanding two-man operation. Those of us who witnessed the change from two to one-man (and woman) bus operation, despite the economic sense of it, truly missed the 'service' aspect of someone on hand who could be distracted and involved in conversation. In those days conductors were a role model for children – how many of us were thrilled to receive a conductor's cap and equipment for Christmas – even those of us, who quite definitely wanted to be a bus driver when we grew up!

Above: In 1959, there was a great deal of excitement on the River Mersey when the 'Windsor Castle' was launched from the Cammell Laird shipyard in Birkenhead. After a traumatic and drawn-out demarcation dispute in the yard between unions and employers, some had thought that the ship would never be finished or launched. This graceful, yet compact ship was scheduled to transport mail to South Africa along with a discerning group of passengers enjoying first class accommodation. The 38,000 ton ship, built to sail for the Cunard White Star Line, was the largest to have been built at Cammell Laird since the 'Mauretania', launched in 1938. The attendance of the Queen Mother to launch the ship possibly accounted for a crowd of 50,000 spectators, although many were just relieved to see the finished vessel.

Below: This peaceful evening view of Birkenhead Docks taken in 1958 shows the Royal Liver Building in Liverpool in the background. From the height of its trading activity pre-war in 1939, by the time this picture was taken, world trade had changed with the opening up of new markets and new relationships and with a new world order of marine trading nations. Whilst the Vittoria Dock was expanded in the 1950s to take larger vessels from the Far East, by the mid 1960s, the competition for trade had moved the initiative into the hands of other European ports. In many ways, this photograph subtly captures the quietness starting to descend on the Birkenhead Docks, presenting a prospect of immense change and the need to adapt to new markets and methods to preserve employment for local people.

LOOKING DOWN
The bigger picture

The opportunity to examine an aerial view, of our own location or familiar places, is an exciting prospect, not least because it provides us with a 'context' for a well-known street or building already firmly planted at ground level in our memory. The excitement also comes from accessing a viewpoint that would not be easily available for most of us. In 1903, the Wright brothers had successfully demonstrated the potential of powered flight and lived to tell the tale. The advent of conflict in the shape of World War I created a new and urgent impetus for aviation technology to move on – and quickly. Speed, manoeuvrability and safety were preoccupations for every member of the Royal Flying Corps and their superiors, mainly for purposes of reconnaissance as well as actual combat: knowing where the enemy was, together with its weaponry, defences and its concentration of troops, had long since proved to be an essential part of any conflict. From the time of the Crimean War in the mid-nineteenth century, when photographers such as Roger Fenton had dragged a converted wine merchant's cart cum mobile dark room around the battlefield, photography had advanced to a level of portability and adaptability to cater for different needs. Putting photography and flying together proved a useful marriage of skills for war and peace time.

Right: Hamilton Square in Birkenhead, seen in this photograph in 1921, was first conceived in 1825 and completed with the delayed building of the new Town Hall over sixty years later. Five thousand Birkenhead residents witnessed the opening ceremony in February, 1887. It is fitting that this building more recently has housed the Wirral Museum. Victorians enjoyed the benefit of being surrounded by public buildings which were designed and properly built. Indeed, most buildings of this period incorporated a conscious, aesthetic quality married to focused functional requirements, providing local people with an exciting and, often unexpected, vista. Idly observing the industrial hinterland of a major northern city recently, as my train trundled towards its centre, I was struck by its modern industrial buildings and their utter lack of soul or style, thrown together with uniform metal cladding and laced with plastic trimmings. Areas like this give even the casual observer a miserable visual return on their community. We should be happy that the Victorians, whatever their occasional idiosyncrasies, provided us with a sustainable urban landscape, designed and built with style and hints of the ancient past in its Greco-Roman detail.

This wonderfully graphic aerial shot taken on February 15, 1923, gives us an acute sense of this part of town, with the Town Hall clock tower centre left, Hamilton Square behind, and the ship-strewn docks bottom left: Woodside Railway Station is centre bottom with Woodside Ferry Terminal to its right including trams drawn up on the land-side to take ferry passengers into town.

Bottom: If there is one place on the east coast of the Wirral Peninsular that demands an aerial view it is Wallascy Town Hall. Situated, somewhat bizarrely overlooking Seacombe Promenade and the River Mersey, a good bus ride away from Wallasey Village, the Town Hall foundation stone was laid in 1914. Significant though this date was for the rest of the world, for the grandiose imaginations of the local politicians it was a year when decisions made proved not to be the best.

Firstly, the idea for placing the Town Hall in this position was down to local worthies in the council deciding that it would be a good idea to place this 'important' building in the districts of Egremont or Seacombe, as they were the local areas that provided the 'major gateways to the world' – via the Mersey! Secondly, the timing of the laying of the foundation stone meant that the building spent the first six years requisitioned as a military hospital, assuming its intended role of Town Hall only in November, 1920.

So, what did we end up with? Well, admittedly a beautiful building – particularly when viewed from the air. A building not exactly logically placed in the community it was supposed to serve. An imposing frontage with a dramatic flight of steps down to the promenade and the water's edge, but, guess what – the entrance is round the back – or could that be the front? Even King George V, having graciously offered to lay the foundation stone in 1914, cannot have foreseen the 'right royal fiasco' which would ensue.

Right: At the end of the 1930s, Birkenhead's docks were operating flat out to satisfy demand from all over the world. The timing of the start of World War II, however, disrupted business in almost every area except for the building and repair of fighting ships. At the end of hostilities, Birkenhead began its fight to regain large parts of its pre-war business. The 1950s did see an expansion of shipping activity in the town with the

enlarging of the Vittoria Dock to take larger vessels mainly from East Asia and an increase in the importation of iron ore at Bidston Dock. By the 1960s, however, the world was a different place, offering stiff competition to trade on the Mersey. In this aerial photograph from 1947, Hamilton Square continues to dominate the city's central landscape and there is no evidence of the impending high-rise developments to come in the 1960s. Indeed, for a shipbuilding port thought worthy of attack by the enemy, the town looks remarkably unscathed.

These two pictures of New Brighton were taken in 1919 (left) and 1931 respectively. The picture from 1919 shows a large proportion of the New Brighton Tower still remaining. Construction began in 1896 of the 567 feet tower, was the highest building in the country.

During World War I, the Tower was closed to the public and poor maintenance meant that, by 1919, rust had taken hold and the only solution was to dismantle it. The ballroom in the substantial base of the tower remained and, in the sixties, hosted famous stars such as The Beatles, in concert.

In the photograph from 1919, the Royal Liver Building can be clearly seen in the top right of the picture on the Liverpool side of the Mersey. Being so close to Liverpool and with its own ferry terminal it is easy to see why New Brighton became popular in the middle of the twentieth century for the people of Liverpool as a convenient and easy to reach destination. Following its original development as an elegant resort in the first half of the nineteenth century, the second half of the century saw it re-defined as a more affordable destination, with many of the larger houses converted into hotels for visitors.

By the late 1960s, the resort had lost some of its appeal, and with the ending of the ferry service in 1971 and the consequent dismantling of the pier and landing stage, the resort entered a thirty year period of relative decline and inactivity.

Many visitors over previous years will, no doubt, have vivid memories of the resort and its attractions although, sadly, many of these attractions are no longer there.

Right: Seacombe had hosted a ferry terminal of sorts from the middle of the seventeenth century and a hundred years later had evolved into a substantial shipbuilding centre on the Mersey. In the centre left of this picture, taken in 1933, we can see the small station that was established in the 1890s; a planned permanent station tucked up next to the ferry terminal never materialised. Whilst there were regular passenger connections to both ends of the Wirral, including Chester, the line was always biased towards goods traffic and, in 1938, when much of the rest of the local railway network was electrified, this relatively insignificant branch line was excluded from the process. Passenger services continued until 1960 and goods trains for a little longer, before final closure came in the summer of 1963.

Below: This later photograph, taken from the opposite direction in the late 1960s, shows the space in the right foreground where the railway station used to be before excavations began to create the entrance to the Kingsway Tunnel in 1971, offering a second vehicle route under the Mersey into Liverpool. We can also see the indiscriminate Sixties housing development immediately to the left and in front of the Seacombe Ferry terminal

These two aerial views of the Woodside Ferry Terminal were probably taken in the early 1960s as we can still see the railway station to the right of the ferry terminal in both of the pictures. The station was opened in 1870, providing a direct line to London Paddington, courtesy of the Great Western Railway. It closed in 1967 and was demolished a couple of years later. The ferry terminal had also served for many years as an appropriately convenient tram and bus terminus. The first street tramway in Europe, developed by an American called Train – yes really! - ran from Woodside to Birkenhead Park. Although originally horse-drawn, this must have provided a fantastic and unique experience for local people. From 1901 until their early demise in 1937, the trams were electrified. The opening of a new bus station in the town in the 1990s brought an end to the importance of Woodside as a transport terminal, releasing it into the less frenetic world of local tourist attractions.

Above: Aproposal was put forward in 1860 to create a shipping channel from the River Mersey inland to Manchester. By 1776 it was possible for small ships to sail from the Irish Sea to quays at Water Street, in Manchester. A hundred years later, in 1870, economic conditions in Manchester had deteriorated, trade was poor and all the usual consequences of poverty were taking their toll. With strong interest from Daniel Adamson, a Manchester manufacturer, in collaboration with two civil engineers and despite substantial opposition from the city of Liverpool and the railway companies, an enabling Act of Parliament made its way onto the statute books in 1885. With substantial support from small shareholders, a large proportion of the necessary finance was raised by 1887, enabling construction to begin. The Ship Canal was finally completed and filled with water in 1893 and opened to traffic in January, 1894. The end result was a canal which is only slightly shorter than the Panama Canal and the eighth longest ship canal in the world. Its completion resulted in Manchester's economic recovery, further development and the city becoming Britain's third busiest port, despite lying 40 miles from the open sea. Despite its important and illustrious history, the recent development of Salford Docks into a residential and office/retail enclave demanded that ships unload alongside the Canal in Trafford Park, and with a changed emphasis in maritime traffic the Ship Canal today has a more limited role.

Below: Whilst appearing in the Domesday Book, the village of Heswall only began to grow towards the end of the nineteenth century with the opening of two railway lines, one from Bidston to Wrexham Central and the other on the West Kirby to Hooton line, which closed to passengers in 1956. Separated from the eastern banks of the River Dee by an area of heath land, the town became an attractive residential area for Liverpool businessmen to retreat to. This view, taken in 1922, shows the village before its expansion into the small town of over 7,000 residents which it has become today.

Technical Demolition Services Limited
From Railway Sleepers to World Leaders

Technical Demolition Services Limited, based in Wirral, is an independent, privately owned, limited company and has developed into a major international organisation, specialising in demolition, dismantling, asbestos removal and land remediation. The company has acquired substantial and diverse experience, bringing together knowledgable directors and senior managers to form a highly specialised and experienced management team, able to handle large and complex demolition projects across the UK, Europe and around the globe.

Tony Taperell is the founder, Chairman and Managing Director of Technical Demolition Services Ltd. Although Tony was born in London, he moved to Yorkshire with his parents and started in business in 1964. He bought old railway sleepers directly from British Rail for a shilling each and purchased a secondhand saw bench from an old clog mill for £5 together with a van for £15. Taking the back mudguard off the van, he put a belt around the

tyre to the saw bench, put the van into reverse gear and started sawing. Chopping up each sleeper produced enough logs to fill three bags: he would then replace the mudguard and drive the van around the district, selling the logs at 2 shillings and sixpence per bag. This was his first enterprise!

His first wagon was a 1947 Austin Tipper, costing the princely sum of £20, with no electric starter but provided with an old fashioned and somewhat lethal starting handle. A year later, Tony's son was born and was christened Austin. He has worked alongside his father throughout his working life and is now Projects Director for the company.

When Dr. Beeching's infamous axe fell on Britain's rail infrastructure, Tony recognised this as an opportunity and his first demolition project was to take down a railway station in 1964. From this point onwards he was confident that he would enjoy a successful career path in the demolition industry.

At 21 years of age Tony had 32 second-hand Thames Trader Tippers on his various sites, all bought for about £75 each. He would put them out on hire for the princely sum of £1.1 0 shillings per hour. He paid his drivers, mainly gypsies from the local Romany camps, 7/6d an hour, with a fish and chip meal thrown in at dinner time, we call it lunch today!

Top left: *The 1947 Austin Tipper, Tony's first truck.* ***Left:*** *This picture of Tony cutting a coal shute, which supplied coal to the boilers, was in the days before Health and Safety rules demanded a whole range of protective clothing and accessories.* ***Above:*** *Tony and son Austin on their first tractor.*

Working days were long and hard. Tony would make it his business to go to the Gypsy site at 5:30am to collect the men ready for work. On many mornings he had to go to an old Austin A35 van to literally drag one of the drivers out of bed, while listening to the early morning cursing of his employee Tony would be apologising to the man's wife who lay sleeping in the same bed! Tony would take them home in the evening, the wife from the A35 van would come across and say sorry for not kicking her husband out of the van at 5'o clock. We would have a cup of tea while sitting on fallen trees, throw horse shoes or jump on a couple of ponies and race bareback around a farmer's field, something out of Heartbeat maybe?

In the 1970s, Tony, now with Helen, his wife, moved to Wirral to take on a project to demolish 5 Babcock and Wilcox boilers at Bowaters, in Ellesmere Port.

During this project, Tony decided to not only make Wirral his business base but also his family home. Later family additions to the Technical Demolition Services workforce included his twin grandsons, Mark and Lee.

This was not, however, the Taperell family's first taste of life in Wirral. In the early 1930s, Tony's grandfather had been General Foreman on the construction of the Queensway Tunnel under the Mersey, cementing an early connection to the area.

Nearly 60 years later, in 1988, Technical Demolition Services moved into a magnificent building at 17, Hamilton Square, Birkenhead. Intrigued as to the history of the building, the company traced the previous tenants of the building through the census records held in the Wirral Museum. In the mid-nineteenth century, shortly after the creation of Hamilton Square and its fine buildings, an Irish wine merchant resided at number 17, complete with Irish staff and servants. Ten years later, number 17 was home to a dentist and his Irish wife and family.

The Irish connection was maintained, as the company, from its Wirral Head Office, competed fiercely and successfully for the contract to demolish the famous shipbuilding yard of Harland and Wolff, based in Belfast, Northern Ireland. This was the yard which had built the ill-fated liner, the Titanic. Having

Top left: *Tony (the one in the tie) and his gypsy crew on site at the Bowaters project in the 1970s.* **Above:** *Tony's grandfather W. Iles, middle row fifth from left, pictured during the Mersey Tunnel ventilation experiments in 1931.* **Left:** *TDS's 17 Hamilton Square Head Office.* **Below:** *Harland and Wolff, Belfast, was another demolition contract won by the company.*

Just as John Laird, whilst residing at number 63, Hamilton Square, held a vision of striving for continuous improvement of his surrounding area, so Tony Taperell and all those working at Technical Demolition Services mirror that ideal today. As Chairman of the Birkenhead Improvement Commission, Laird played a key role in the development of the town. Throughout Technical Demolition Services' history they have ensured that demolition is not a finite ending to a once loved building, structure, landmark or residential property, but an exciting venture enabling regeneration, new life and opportunities for the people of Wirral. Technical Demolition Services are aware of the impact its range of services can have upon the redevelopment and regeneration of areas. Decontamination and remediation of heavy industrial-use land is a key factor where land is a high value commodity. A 25 acre site located in Bromborough, Wirral, was an ex-M.O.D. Reserve Fuel Storage Depot, consisting of nine earth-concealed fuel storage tanks, a manifold pit station, pump house, pits and below-ground pipe work. The underground tanks and associated pipe work had performed a strategic role in Britain's war effort. Operation PLUTO

successfully bid for all six phases of this £5 million shipyard project, Technical Demolition Services demolished, in total, 6 million square feet of the shipbuilding and repairs complex, together with offices, dockyard cranes and even the on-site mortuary. The company were delighted to be invited by The Titanic Society, to its celebration dinner, marking the 90th anniversary of the construction of the Titanic. The event was held at Belfast City Hall in period costume.

Proud to have moved into prestigious Hamilton Square, built originally by the shipbuilding magnate, John Laird, it seems somehow fitting that Technical Demolition Services pioneered U.K. ship dismantling from this site. On February 12th, 2007, the Ministry of Defence announced that H.M.S Intrepid would be the very first Royal Navy ship to be recycled at a British facility. Technical Demolition Services, in partnership with Leavesley International, were honoured to be uniquely selected as preferred bidder, chosen for this historic and momentous mission to demolish the vessel under the DEFRA Guidelines for 'Safe and Environmentally Sound Recycling of Ships'.

Top: The demolition of H.M.S Intrepid. The very first Royal Navy ship to be recycled. Right: The ex-M.O.D Reserve Fuel Storage Depot at Bromborough, Wirral.

men. On the day that demolition work began, in 1984, a kestrel's nest, containing chicks, was discovered in the cab of one of the cranes, halting the project for six weeks as the chicks were allowed to grow. The R.S.P.B. monitored the fledglings and, later, when caught and released as mature birds in the Lake District, a bronze medal for animal life-saving was awarded to the foreman on the Birkenhead site.

(Pipe-Lines Under The Ocean), was a World War II operation by British scientists, oil companies and armed forces to construct undersea oil pipelines under the English Channel between England and France. Allied forces on the European continent required enormous amounts of fuel.

This is to certify that the of THE ROYAL SOCIETY FOR THE PREVENTION OF CRUELTY TO ANIMALS has been awarded to

The Stone Manganese Marine Company, based in Birkenhead docks, was a manufacturer of propellers for more than 100 years and one of the largest in the world. The company was able to produce propellers with a finished weight of over 100 tonnes. When the company closed its doors for the last time, Technical Demolition Services were awarded the contract to demolish the warehouses and offices. The workshops were left as if the engineers were still employed there, with many drawings, tools and instruments of their trade remaining in situ. It is interesting to speculate as to whether they were the manufacturers of the propellers for the Titanic.

During the company's demolitions and excavations, it was possible to appreciate at first hand, the sheer ingenuity of those responsible for the original construction of this particular site, together with the bravery, cunning and determination of all those involved with Operation PLUTO. Along with the Mulberry Harbours, which were constructed immediately after D-Day, Operation PLUTO must surely be considered as one of history's greater feats of military engineering.

Western Ship Repairers, based in Birkenhead, was a massive company in its heyday, employing hundreds of

Technical Demolition Services have demolished 14 tower blocks over the years, dramatically changing the face of Wirral. The demolition of the finance building, which was a multi-storey office block on Cleveland Street, Birkenhead, was a challenging project, as it included a requirement that the ground floor should be left intact, for re-use once the contract was completed. The

Top: *The first day of demolition at Western Ship Repairers in 1984 uncovered a nest of kestrels in the cab of one of the cranes. Pictured are the chicks and the bronze medal certificate awarded to the foreman of the Birkenhead site.* **Left:** *Stages of demolition of the office block on Cleveland Street, Birkenhead.*

Club, and the company was inundated with fans requesting memorabilia, especially bricks from the Cowshed Stand, for use as door stops.

The company has demolished over 2,000 terraced properties within the Birkenhead area, looking to the future by regenerating and providing better standards of living for local residents.

The New Dock Hotel, known locally as 'The Blood Tub', was demolished recently by the company. It stood near to the Laird's complex called

foreman received many requests for jobs from local men, one of whom, on hearing that one floor was to be left intact, enquired which floor!

Following the tragedy at Hillsborough football ground, new legislation came into force requiring allocated seating for all fans. Technical Demolition Services were awarded the contract to demolish the stands at Tranmere Rovers Football

*Above: Demolition of the stands at Tranmere Rovers Football Ground. **Below:** The two 1950s dockside cranes in Birkenhead which were brought to earth one Sunday morning in 2009.*

the Dock Cottages and opposite Arthur H. Lee's Tapestry Works, which had been much loved by Birkenhead residents for many years.

Technical Demolition Services were responsible for the façade retention and internal demolition of the old grain silos at Spillers Mills. Spillers the Millers were not only a huge employer in Wirral, but a nationwide and worldwide company, eventually bought out by Rank Hovis McDougall. The mill has been preserved and converted into luxury apartments as part of the on-going development of the dockside area.

In 2009, at 8 a.m. on a Sunday morning, two dockside cranes in Birkenhead were brought to earth using explosives demolition. The cranes dated back to the 1950s when the dockyards were still thriving. Just as they had stood by each other, like sisters, for over 40 years, so they fell, gracefully together, providing locals with an early morning alarm call.

The success of the company has enabled the business to evolve into a worldwide operation, with contracts as far away as Cyprus, Spain and their ship recycling operations in Jeddah, Saudi Arabia, although the heart of the company remains in Birkenhead, bringing employment to generations of Wirral residents. The management team has grown with the company but still works out of the Head Office in Hamilton Square, overseeing and monitoring all on-going and future contracts.

In 2009, Technical Demolition Services was nominated and short-listed for the International Demolition Awards, held in Amsterdam and is still, currently, in the top 100 worldwide demolition companies. The company recently invested in new business premises, centrally located near to Birkenhead and Wallasey Docks, to house its plant, workshop and maintenance staff, ensuring that all operations still remain within Wirral.

Top left: Tony Taperell (right) and Austin Taperell (left) receive a 5 Star Award from the British Safety Council on behalf of Technical Demolition Services Limited. *Left:* Members of the board, 2009. *Above:* Helen and Tony Taperell, 2009.

DAYS TO REMEMBER
With joy and sadness

Celebration is important in our lives, including the celebration in mourning the lives of those no longer with us. The opportunity to celebrate with family and friends often adds to the joy of the occasion, be it a one-off or a regularly repeated event. Expression of our joy in celebration often provides the antidote to more sober and less happy occasions. Royal visits were always 'special', particularly for local children; the magic of being able to stand close to a 'real live' Queen was straight out of a story book! Indeed, before the advent of television for all and red-top media obsession with 'celebrity', London, Buckingham Palace and the Royal Family were part of every child's mythology rather than part of their everyday reality. Not least because of their rarity, these visits were interpreted by individuals as a very personal act of support and a positive gesture to the community.

Left: The original plans for the construction of Hamilton Square, laid down in the early 1800s included a piece of land set aside for the building of the Town Hall. Eventually, a design by Charles Ellison, a local architect, was agreed upon with construction completed in 1887. This photograph, taken in the early 1880s, shows the laying of the foundation stone. Whilst still owned by the local council, the building has not been used as the Town Hall since the early 1990s. After some restoration, the building became the site for the Wirral Museum and also accommodates the Assembly Rooms.

Above: This picture shows King George V arriving at Hooton Station in 1913 on a visit to Port Sunlight, the model village created by William Hesketh Lever in 1888 to house workers at his soap factory. As an admired and philanthropic industrialist, Lord Leverhulme, as he later became, enjoyed the respect of many, including the Royal Family. By demonstrating his respect in this way, the King was able to show, by reflection, his respect for the working people of his country.

Above: From 1914, Britain was thrown into the conflict of The Great War. As a major builder and repairer of ships, the importance of the Cammell Laird Shipyard during the two world wars was immense. The ability of the workers to build new or replacement ships and to repair ships damaged in the conflict as quickly as possible, was a major contribution to the war effort. Ever mindful of the impact of his support, particularly in the gloom of wartime conditions, King George V, seen here visiting the yard in 1917, showed a tireless commitment in supporting the working population.

Right: In recent times, Royal visits have often included a 'walkabout', designed to further encourage a perceived closeness of members of the Royal family to their subjects. Sometimes it works, sometimes it doesn't, with the ever-present threat of terrorism making it difficult to 'police' this closeness.

In July, 1934, when this photograph was taken, the proximity of ordinary people to the Royal visitors depended entirely on their rank, elected position or particular social standing. The relationship was, however, important to the men and women in the street, who revered the leadership and example which royalty presented and were openly patriotic at the drop of a hat. It could be said that the expansionist ambitions which created the Empire under Queen Victoria imbued a degree of gratitude for the increased wealth, employment and opportunities which this activity brought to the country. Despite the profound loss of life and the subsequent fracturing of family life during World War I and after, the positives were perceived to outweigh the negatives.

Here, you can almost feel the restraint which has been exercised from the moment the royal Daimler slid to a halt in front of the waiting dignitaries. It is clear that King George V and Queen Mary were welcomed to the throne in 1911 and, loved by the nation, not least after revoking their Germanic titles and connections as they created the House of Windsor. Whether real or postured, it was rumoured that the King frequently expressed his xenophobia and his dislike of anything 'foreign'! How difficult the First World War must have been, a nightmare you would not have wished on any family: one first cousin was Kaiser Wilhelm II of Germany, otherwise known as 'the enemy' and the other first cousin was Tsar Nicholas II of Russia, whose continued presence prompted the Russian Revolution which was to dictate the agonisingly fraught and cold century which lay ahead for the Russian people. The demand and expectation that, as a Royal or relevant aristocrat, you would marry to or above your station, allowed for the union of cousins and the unspoken insistence that you first checked out your own extended family and other likely and wealthy families of influence across the civilised world before you succumbed to love, was understood by most.

As we can see, from the top left of this photograph, many residents of Birkenhead turned out for the opening of their spacious new library in Borough Road, still successfully ploughing its furrow today.

Today, Mayors and Mayoresses are largely ceremonial figures, but in wartime and the austerity of the post-war decades, they assumed a greater and high profile role as leaders of the community and were looked up to with great respect. In these two pictures, William Short and his wife, Mayor and Mayoress respectively of Birkenhead when photographed in June, 1953, demonstrate their support

for the people of their community as they celebrate the first real high point in the life of Britain after the Second World War, namely the coronation of our present monarch, Queen Elizabeth II.

The Mayor is seen cutting the cake at the Coronation Party in St. Stephen's Church Hall, on June 5. Having already enjoyed an enormous street party on Coronation Day, three days earlier, local families demonstrated their unrestrained appetite for cakes, buns, jelly and other delightful morsels, glad to push the deprivation and restrictions of wartime and the rationing that followed, behind them. Once the feverish consumption of jellies was complete, such an enormous gathering of children had, of course, to be entertained. So all the fun of those activities still referred to as parlour games began and, no doubt, continued long into the evening.Three days earlier, the Lady Mayoress performed the reflective and symbolic crowning of the local Festival Queen, on a somewhat rudimentary stage set up in the car park of the Ritz. As we can see, the girls loved this kind of event, feeling 'royal' for a day made you feel special, after all. The boys, however, don't look quite as pleased and were probably quick to hide away their copy of the photograph of this 'happy' day or were made to cringe for the next five years every time 'mum' pulled out the family album to show everyone what wonderful events had embraced them as a growing boy. Still, mum always knew best, didn't she?

Below: The street parties that were held all over the country, including the Wirral, on VE Day in 1945 were a way for families, friends and neighbours to show their relief at the end of a long and bitter conflict. At that time, families were also mourning the loss of those who did not return and were still awaiting their reunion with those who would return. The celebration of our current monarch's Silver Jubilee, in 1977, also prompted a further baking of fairy cakes and jam tarts, the dragging out of every available church hall trestle table and the collecting of every child in sight. As we can see in this picture, compared to 1945 there was, at least, a little more obviously unrestrained happiness. This party was held in Charlotte Road, Wallasey on 6 June, 1977.

Above: The opening of the Trevor Lloyd Hughes Spastics Centre, at Clatterbridge, was an important event at Clatterbridge Hospital in 1966. An invitation to HRH Princess Marina, Duchess of Kent, was accepted and in October, 1966, she duly arrived to fulfil the engagement. She appears to be sharing a moment of concern with the gentleman on the left over the function of the button on the wall. What was likely to happen if she pushed it? Presumably everything occurred that was meant to occur and the centre was successfully opened.

Princess Marina was a constantly busy and respected Royal, who had married the Duke of Kent in 1934. She came from a Russian, Danish and Greek background but settled comfortably and quickly into British royalty. Tragically, her married life lasted for a mere eight years, as the Duke was killed in a 'plane crash whilst on active service with the RAF in August, 1942, six weeks after the birth of their second son, Prince Michael. Her quiet and consistent support for many organisations and charities rightly earned her the respect of the nation. The Princess sadly passed away from a brain tumour in August, 1961.

This page: Royal visits were usually welcomed and put a smile on people's faces. Sometimes events of history conspired to compromise the happiness and joy expected

of such an event. Having experienced considerable industrial strife through the late 1950s, despite the contract to build the 'Ark Royal' aircraft carrier and several tankers for the burgeoning oil industry, the fifties and sixties had been punctuated by industrial action, emphasising the changing nature of the industry. There were also regular stand-offs between employers and unions representing the interests of the workers. In this photograph, the picket line at Western Ship Repairers emphasises the strong feelings of workers and those facing unemployment from the company. The calls for nationalisation referred to the fact that the Cammell Laird yard had been nationalised in 1977 as British Shipbuilders. The opposition at a Royal visit at this time in 1978 is plain to see. Despite this, HRH Princess Anne seems relatively unperturbed, mingling with crowds of women, children and some men at the Cammell Laird yard. The Princess had long since developed a recognisably stoical response to awkward moments such as this and the smile remained to gladden the hearts of some.

Arrowe Hall was built in Arrowe Park in 1835 by John Shaw, who had inherited the land which his uncle had bought at the turn of the nineteenth century. Having built the hall, John Shaw constructed an impressive country estate with landscaped park land and accommodation for estate workers. Through the further ownership of a Captain Shaw and later, Lord Leverhulme, the estate was eventually sold to Birkenhead Corporation in the mid-1920s and in 1974 transferred to the newly-formed Metropolitan Borough of Wirral. In 1982, Arrowe Park Hospital was built on a 15 acre site in the park. The hospital was officially opened by Queen Elizabeth II on the 4 May, 1982. In these photographs we see the arrival of the Queen and her presentation to a line of excited staff and also her meeting with a young patient of the new hospital – this time, smiles all round.

STREET WISE
a change of view

Over a hundred year period, our streets have changed out of all recognition. On the death of Queen Victoria in 1901 after a sixty three year reign, streets were empty of motorised traffic; horses, bicycles and feet were the order of the day.

Women at the turn of the twentieth century wore ankle-length coats and dresses. At this time, the opposite gender truly believed that women 'moved in a mysterious way', which in fact they did: from the waist down, women were an enigma, their shape and movement a total mystery to any observer, welcome or not. Horses had long been a possible form of personal transport for women since the invention of the side saddle but, for a long time, the bicycle presented an insurmountable – or should that be un-mountable - problem; the 'ladies crossbar' did not cope entirely successfully with the long and heavy material of women's clothing. Ladies stepped in and out of horse-drawn cabs and carriages for another twenty years until, in the mid 1920s, public transport fully embraced the motorised omnibus and created, for these same ladies, wider horizons.

The Victorian era, fuelled by the economic furnace of the Industrial Revolution, had supported the design and building of impressive, grand and glorious public buildings in town and city centres. Newly affluent industrialists saw the opportunity to massage their egos with monuments in stone to their success and achievement. In the twentieth century, with two world wars in relatively swift succession to fund and contend with, rebuilding of public buildings was largely deferred until later in the century, apart, that is, from necessary and urgent renewing of essential buildings destroyed by wartime bombing.

By 1950, as the country dragged itself out of the ruins of a hard fought victory at the end of World War II and prepared to look forward to a 'new beginning', the powers that be, in local and national government set course on an often catastrophic route to urban renewal. As the programme gathered pace during the 1960s, the 'fashion' for redevelopment and renewal spread with unstoppable zeal across the country, with an increase in wealth after post-war austerity. The introduction of new legislation at the end of the 1960s, such as the Listed Buildings Act and Town and City Centre Conservation Areas, sadly came too late to save some of the finest Victorian buildings in our towns and cities, including Birkenhead, thereby changing our urban vistas forever.

Naturally, concern is now expressed that many of the replacement buildings put up in the 1960s and 1970s are already being demolished as they are apparently coming to the end of their time and usefulness! These wholesale changes to the physical make-up of towns and cities succeeded in altering the shape and form of street life, with more big landlords, more chain stores and fewer small private businesses in city centres and a massive increase in personal transportation.

Below: This picture of Seacombe Ferry, taken towards the end of the nineteenth century, shows the simple architectural elegance of the terminal building. Amazingly, ferries had crossed the River Mersey from Seacombe since the middle of the seventeenth century although a regular and reliable service, complete with timetable, only arrived 60-70 years before this photograph was taken. The introduction of the 'Etna', a steam paddle boat, in 1817, revolutionised the ferry service for the next 100 years or so, as steamers were able to combat the vagaries of wind and tide like never before. The taxis seen here in the form of horses and carriages would know precisely when the next ferry was due to arrive or depart, making the lives of everybody much simpler. That is, until 1934, when the opening of the first Mersey Road Tunnel, The Queensway, would seriously affect ferry traffic. The Mersey Rail Tunnel, opened in 1886, had dealt with the congestion of traffic of people and goods caused by the evolution of industries on both sides of the River. The new road tunnel seriously impacted on goods traffic and with the cessation of the Seacombe 'luggage boats' after World War II, ferry traffic went into a slow tailspin, not helped by the opening of a second road tunnel from Wallasey to Liverpool in 1971. After much soul-searching, it was decided to transform the declining ferry service into a tourist attraction, with the Mersey Ferries Heritage Cruises running from the Seacombe Terminal.

It must have seemed quite unusual in one way, but obvious in another, for your employer to name your district after his company's most famous product. This is what happened in 1899, when William Hesketh Lever, later Lord Leverhulme, decided to create a model village for his employees, next to his soap factory, between Lower Bebington and New Ferry and named it Port Sunlight. When Lever decided to move his soap-making business from Warrington, the place he chose was a 56 acre site, sandwiched between the River Mersey and a railway line. On this marshy piece of land, Lever re-established his factory and set about building a model village between 1899 and 1914, using almost thirty architects to build a total of 800 houses to accommodate a similar number of his workers and their families, providing allotments, schools, a church and a temperance hotel. Lever was keen to promote his own philosophy of learning and life amongst his workers and set up various schemes for their education and welfare. The Lady Lever Art Gallery was established to promote an interest in the arts amongst the residents and to house a substantial art collection from Lord Leverhulme's travels around the world. The gallery is housed in a striking building in the village. The setting for the village reflected the ideas of the Arts and Crafts Movement and of William Morris, which were echoed in the architectural styles and in the detailing of the landscape design. Along with other such model villages at Saltaire and Bourneville, the company had access to a locally-based and contented workforce, fit in mind and body, which enjoyed well-designed, dry and comfortable housing plus numerous well thought out community facilities.

This practical philosophy in staff management proved to be a good investment. It was only in the 1980s that houses were first sold privately. The photographs we see here show the finely detailed main entrance to the company's offices, examples of half-timbered housing in the village - not dissimilar to traditional housing across the County of Cheshire over several hundred years, the village schools in Park Road and the Girls Dining Hall at Hulme Hall, all pictured between 1900 and 1916.

Today, local and national politicians would have you believe that 'slums' do not or barely exist in this country. Some of the elements that existed in the slums of 1900 certainly still *do* occur in some shape or form but it is now probably down to a different degree of poverty. These four pictures, taken around the early 1900s, demonstrate a tangible evidence of poverty and deprivation that would instantly attach the label 'slum' on all these scenes without a second thought. We see the central gutter, the cheap brickwork, the claustrophobic nature of the outdoor corridors and the dilemma of deciding on the worst place to be, indoors or out. Add zero internal sanitation, no effective heating and ventilation, blind ends to alleys with no views, and dangerous and dark underground passages and you would not wish these circumstances on anyone. At the time these pictures were taken, the word 'environment' with all its various connotations had not been invented and if it had, none would have been appropriate or adequate to explain or describe such a squalid apology for housing.

Right: In 1898, Thomas Owen and his family arrived in Birkenhead with their children, of which the eldest was Wilfred. On the death of Wilfred's grandfather in 1897 the family had to leave the family home in Oswestry and move into rented accommodation in Birkenhead, Wilfred's father having accepted a position at Woodside Railway Station. Wilfred attended the Birkenhead Institute and in 1903/1904 the family moved to the house in the photograph, 14 Wilmer Road. For Wilfred, this coincided with a holiday in Cheshire during which he was able to contemplate his Christian beliefs and a future vocation. The holiday also proved to be the genesis of his early thoughts on his own poetry and on the great poets of the day.

After working as a lay assistant at a church near Reading, Wilfred became keenly aware of the chasm that existed between the doctrine and liturgy of the church and the harsh realities of life for the less fortunate. Later, he travelled to France to work as a private tutor in Bordeaux.

In 1915, he enlisted in the Artists' Rifles Officers' Training Corps and trained at a camp in Essex. After commissioning as a second lieutenant in June, 1916, he arrived at the front with an arrogant and detached attitude, particularly in relation to his troops. After suffering two major incidents in the trenches, his views changed and sometime later he was returned to a hospital in Edinburgh with shell shock. His time here introduced him to the poet, Siegfried Sassoon, an experience which catalysed much of his thinking on war and poetry.

Having returned to the front, leading units of the Second Manchester Regiment near Joncourt, Wilfred was tragically killed, just one week before the end of the war. During his

lifetime, only five of his poems had been published. Although, ultimately, considered a greater poet than Sassoon, Wilfred Owen's poetry benefitted from Sassoon's promotion and his editing of Owen's work. His profound and unstintingly graphic ability to translate into poetry the absolute horrors of war can be said to have radically changed the thinking of vast numbers of people over the last eighty years and, on the way, created more than a few pacifists. The reality checks he faced in his own short life were left for a nation to consider, a warning to heed, a reasoning to suppose. It can truly be said that Wilfred Owen left his mark, in print and in the mind of those he left behind.

Bottom left and below: Hoylake has remained a popular, small-scale and somewhat genteel resort placed at the north western tip of the Wirral peninsular for over 200 years. The Royal Hotel was built to attract visitors to the town towards the end of the eighteenth century and vessels travelling between Liverpool and North Wales brought increasing custom to the hotel and the town. With a racecourse constructed in the mid 1800s, in the grounds of The Royal, patronage continued unabated alongside newly arrived residents from the thriving industrial areas of Birkenhead and Liverpool. Market Street, Hoylake, seen here at the turn of the twentieth century and roughly 30 years later, provides an indication of life on small town main streets in the first half of the twentieth century. In the earlier photograph, only horse-drawn vehicles are to be seen and probably, through any given day, the street did not look much busier than this. Local deliveries were usually made with hand or horse pulled carts, speed taking a back seat and friendliness, familiarity and helpfulness sitting proudly up front. Passing the time of day with others whilst standing in the roadway was perfectly normal and safe; after all, there were few things faster than a pedestrian at this time. Motor power, attached to both cars and buses, brought a new sharpness and awareness to simple tasks such as crossing the road, although the young mum on the left of the picture, with her massive and not so wieldy coachbuilt, four-wheeled baby carrier, would *not* require a pedestrian crossing and would glide easily to the other side of the street with adequate safety and just a little common sense.

Left: The hydraulic tower at Birkenhead Dock was a casualty of German bombing during World War II. Built in 1863, it was in the style of the Florentine building, Piazza Della Signoria. The area of Northern Italy, between Florence and Siena, provided the inspiration for many decorative towers in the latter half of the nineteenth century. An excellent remaining example can be seen at Grimsby on the east coast, overlooking the entrance to the dock area. As a major shipbuilding town, Birkenhead was an obvious target for the Luftwaffe, and bombing raids began in August, 1940, with a servant girl living in Prenton becoming the first casualty. Under the onslaught of 11 raids during September, everybody rushed off to their domestic brick shelters or their Morrison indoor shelters, or best of all to the 6,000 Anderson shelters. Living in an industrial environment, you had to accept that these were the areas which would be targeted. Any vaguely industrial company with engineering capabilities would inevitably find itself pulled into the war effort, making and repairing the machinery of wartime and using a largely female workforce to do so. The damage of retaliation was inevitable, in some areas profound and tragic, in others, not as severe as had been expected. But it was still a very long six years.

Top: When World War II darkened our skies in 1939, the need for the whole country to be watchful for airborne intruders was matched by the demand for those on the ground to be able to manage the impact of the enemy and to protect all aspects of life from potential devastation. ARP (Air Raid Precautions) had been set up in the United Kingdom fifteen years earlier to anticipate the possible threat from the newly developed bomber aircraft. It was not so much a feeling that a war was imminent, but a realisation that the advanced industrial world had invented yet another potentially devastating machine of mass destruction without thinking to invent, simultaneously, another machine or method as an antidote. The first task of wardens was to patrol the streets during the 'blackout', making sure that no light could be seen, as well as ensuring incendiary devices were rendered harmless. They operated alongside the police in managing emergency situations, particularly where bomb damage had occurred and they were well trained in fire-fighting and first aid. Most ARP wardens were volunteers and many of them had full-time day jobs. There were nearly 1.4 million ARP wardens in the country during the war, but as a result of call-ups, injury and demand a constant and on-going campaign of recruitment was necessarily in operation throughout the war. This photograph, taken somewhere in Birkenhead during the early years of the war, shows a mobile advertising vehicle, reminding the population that their gas masks should always be 'to hand'. Forgotten heroes of the ARP were the teenagers used as runners and messengers during air raids, in the absence of consistent and reliable radio and other telecommunications. The efforts and commitment of these 14-18 year olds were no less admirable and brave than the efforts of the ARP wardens themselves.

Above: The 1950s, when this photograph of Hamilton Square Station was taken, still came under the umbrella of the steam age in railway terms, providing a diverse, useful and necessary facility across the whole Wirral Peninsular as well as under the River Mersey to Liverpool. The true advent of 'personal transport' only increased its grip on the population at large at the end of the decade and Hamilton Square continued to disgorge its mass of workers, on a daily basis, into the streets of Birkenhead. Even a mere 10-12 years before the demise of steam, the railways and their monstrous, steaming locomotives continued to bewitch younger and older enthusiasts, with their pads, pencils, sandwiches and anoraks. Train-spotting continued into the diesel/electric era but, somehow, without the mechanical kerfuffle, the smells and the magnificent enormity of these iron horses it was never quite the same again.

Right: Victorian architecture has often been derided, particularly in the early and mid-1960s when the desire to move quickly away from the dull and sluggish post-war years gave an aggressive, and often, quality-free, approach to the re-building of towns and cities across the country. Much of the architecture of the nineteenth century, fuelled by the wealth and drive of the Industrial Revolution, created a remarkable variety of classically styled and substantial buildings which also gave substance and integrity to many town and city

centres. This renaissance in public building coincided with the formalising of the profession of landscape architecture and a willingness of town and city authorities and architects to recognise the potential for providing pleasant parks and building-free areas in the middle of the bustle, industry and, occasionally, insanitary conditions in which people still lived and worked. The POS was born! Public Open Spaces appeared from the early 1800s onwards, initially as a visual, active and prestigious massage of a town's ambitions. Birkenhead was fortunate in benefitting from the sound relationship between the entrepreneur William Laird and the architect James Gillespie Graham, and their desire to dramatically improve the heart of the town. The result was Hamilton Square, begun in 1826 and completed nearly sixty years later, an open space to be proud of and, at the time, considered to be one of the finest town centre spaces in the whole of Europe. This view, taken in 1959, shows clearly the broad public walkways, carefully arranged tree planting and an open expanse of grass enabling full view of the vista provided by the impressive Victorian public and private buildings on the perimeter of the square. How grateful we should be to the architects and entrepreneurs of Victorian times for providing the town with this long-standing and useable contribution to public and daily life.

In the 1950s, Hamilton Square had traffic flowing through it all day, every day, long before it became the quiet parking backwater that it has become now. The lad on the left appears to have been put in charge of his little sister while mum popped into a local office or business; he seems happy to face the camera and to do his duty, although his friend appears to resent the interruption to more essential, important and pressing 'boys time'.

future should be assured as an integral part of the town's history. We often find it too easy to sweep away the glories of our urban history in a crazed search for something new and better without always ensuring the security of some of our best existing buildings and without striving for the similarly appropriate aesthetic and functional elegance which was evident in earlier times.

Above: The 'late arrival' of the Town Hall to Hamilton Square, in Birkenhead, was eagerly awaited, completing, a fine set of buildings surrounding the square vested with the appropriate degree of dignity and imposition to ensure that they would still be admired a hundred and thirty years later. Hopefully, the changed priorities and requirements of local councils will not affect the future use and ownership of this building. As a magnificent example of nineteenth century civic architecture its

Below: In many ways, 1950 should have been the beginning of 'something new', following the aftermath of World War II. In reality, moving investment, industry and people's lives forward at an acceptable and noticeable pace took a little longer to sort out. The values and landscapes had, generally, not changed in 1950. Cars were being produced again, but with the old dies of pre-war models they were new but, actually more of the same. There was also the issue of customers; after the poverty of war, returning soldiers looking for work and families fragmented through bereavement and separation, this was not exactly an economy brimming with confidence and ready to 'splash the cash'. This view of Argyle Street South,

looking towards Borough Road and the centre of Birkenhead, has an almost ghostly aspect with snow and frost and a lack of cars. The cars we see in the distance are almost certainly black in colour; it took another five years of production and the introduction of newer, more fashionable models to bring in fresh colours such as, cardigan beige, midnight blue and bottle green.

The uniformity of streets like Argyle Street South were a familiar site in every industrial town, unpretentious terraced housing with a minimum of facilities, no garden and a back yard. They enabled town centre workers to live within walking or cycling distance of centres of work, obviating the need for personal transport, apart from a bicycle. One thing this kind of housing did offer was a closeness to others and the potential of a vibrant and tightly-knit community. Ultimately, the razing of such properties, in this case, to make way for a flyover, was seen as an improvement at the time. Replacement accommodation did not always include the potential to continue these close relationships, even if you did end up with a modern heating system and an inside toilet. Progress was relative, however, and new pre-occupations meant that we demanded different things as we staggered into 'the light' of the sixties, with all its craziness, bright colours and inappropriate relationships. But a cup of sugar, somehow, was never quite the same again.

Right: Once the poverty of the immediate post-war years yielded to a necessary move forward, there was a mad dash by local councils to build-anew, often without the realisation of what they were removing as the first step. Like many other industrial towns and cities around the country a new beginning was required, sooner rather than later, and the loaded gun of progress was a potent weapon to be aimed at local councils. The new entrepreneurs emerging after World War II also wanted progress and, occasionally, were prepared to sacrifice reality and quality on the altar of profit and expansion.

The area around Oak and Eldon Gardens was a typical industrial residential landscape and needed change. This photograph taken in 1978, as the 'new' flats were being pulled to the ground, also gives us a glimpse of what this block replaced. Yes, it replaced damp, poorly heated and ventilated housing with no inside sanitation: but it also replaced a closeness and intimacy and the possibility to practise this but failed to replace it with anything with a similarly positive impact. One of the major differences between this

country and others, in terms of capital investment on major building projects is the principle of excluding future maintenance from the capital cost. For the developer, this makes for a lower budget but it also often means that the quality of all materials used in the building are not considered from the point of view of reliability and longevity. In other words, after twenty years a building poorly constructed from the cheapest materials may well have deteriorated to such an extent that it is not feasible for it to be properly repaired. We have regularly seen the demolition of hundred-year-old buildings across the country largely on the basis of them being no longer 'fit for purpose'. These buildings are often still solid and in excellent condition for their age, yet they are pulled down and replaced with new buildings, less well built and less aesthetically pleasing, which themselves are ready for replacement 20-30 years into their life. Sad, then, that architects, planners and developers often seem unwilling to use their skills to adapt and re-form older buildings for further use rather than lose these icons of our local history largely for the sake of building something new.

Above: Corporation Road, Birkenhead, connecting Hoylake Road to Vittoria Dock, seen here in 1953, is full of the hustle and bustle of the day, with a line of traffic pausing as the rag and bone man gently encourages his horse into a tight right turn. Until the late 1960s, rag and bone men were the recyclers of the day and have been around for as long as our parents and grandparents can remember, clip-clopping along the cobbled streets, down the alleys of our industrial towns and cities, eyeing up the discarded and neglected ephemera of people's back yards. Fifty years ago, rag and bone men were collecting discarded clothing and sending it out to India for the use of the needy there. By the end of the fifties, as austerity slid slowly out of sight and some ten years since their last 'good buy', people stepped out to their local clothing store with the intention of bringing a little colour into their wardrobe. So that lovely dark grey best woollen suit you'd bought in 1937 found its way onto a boat destined for the Indian sub-continent! The regularity with which these men, with their faithful and obedient horses, travelled around the same route in each district was an encouragement to move on to the beckoning future rather than remain stuck in the lingering past. For children, there was sometimes a balloon to look forward to, for them a welcome distraction, to mums merely bribery and incentive to spring clean *every* week! Looking to the left of the picture, after a quick 'hello, hello, what 'ave we 'ere?', we manage to work out that it's a policeman, in the street, on duty, a sight

almost forgotten today. In those days, the policeman had his beat, kept 'an eye on things' and had time for a friendly chat – how things have changed. A small Austin truck heads the queue of waiting traffic with another Austin at the back, the ubiquitous FX3 taxi, sandwiching a Scammell tractor unit, used widely at the time for deliveries from railway stations and for other local deliveries where a tight-turning vehicle was essential, and a Hillman Minx, a new post-war shape, but still in black; the Mark Two Minx came in lighter and brighter colours, including a 'de luxe' model called the Californian with a two-tone colour scheme as standard. With television still in its relative infancy, advertising hoardings were a very important way for companies to target their potential customers; fifty years later and Smarties are still there.

Top rightt This view from Holts Hill across town and river, taken in 1972, still highlights the dock area and reminds us on what the Merseyside edge of the Wirral's wealth was based. In the background, we glimpse again the towering architecture of the Royal Liver Building on the Liverpool side of the River Mersey.

Right: The narrow stretch of water, the River Mersey, between Liverpool and Birkenhead has witnessed continuous crossings since the monks of Birkenhead Priory first felt the need to spread

their cassocks. Amazingly, due in no short measure to the forward-thinking attitude by the railway companies in the first 40 years of their existence, the pressure to build a tunnel under the River Mersey had already arrived by the 1870s and by 1886 the Mersey Railway Tunnel was completed, dramatically impacting on the development and population growth of the Wirral Peninsular. With the introduction of the road tunnels, the Queensway from Birkenhead to Liverpool in 1934 and the Kingsway Tunnel from Wallasey to Liverpool in 1971, creating space for the toll booths and the funnelling of traffic into a wide approach concourse required sound thinking and consideration of the back-up effect on the rest of the town's traffic. Flyovers were a necessity to create the space required and this picture, taken in 1974, shows the tunnel approach roads near Birkenhead Central Station, with the historic Edward VII Memorial Clock, erected in 1912, on the left.

Above: This photograph of Whitby Road, Ellesmere Port, was taken in 1961, a year before the opening of the massive Vauxhall Motors factory, which provided an instant increase in job opportunities in the district. The town has grown continuously since the turn of the twentieth century through general industry and dock activity. By the time this photograph was taken, the memory of post-war austerity was slipping away into the mists of time. Good employment opportunities and new fashion and styles in the shops added to a new musical optimism cradled on nearby Merseyside, and there were suddenly good reasons to 'pop to town', splash the cash and plan that trip with the girls to the nearest local nightspot. Tolls Department Store was typical of the town centre business that had steadily expanded until the post-war years when increased competition, as more people gained access to personal transport and a wider choice of shops, brought the reality of such enterprises into sharp relief. It was only another fifteen to twenty years before the impending threat posed by out-of-town shopping parks was to send such stores into a fatal tailspin to oblivion – sad, as many of these stores were family owned by local people. The Queens, on the left, had been showing films for over fifty years at the time this photograph was taken. This week's epic? Why, it's that tall dark stranger with a charismatic name and somewhat limited acting ability, yet again playing his handsome self in 'Hannibal' – bet the elephants weren't looking forward to him taking his shirt off – again.

Below: This photograph of Ellesmere Port railway station, on the left, shows two of the most popular public service vehicles of the 1950s and 1960s, the Austin FX3 taxi and the ubiquitous Bristol Lodekka double-decker bus. On the right we can see the 'cattle arch' which, in olden days, enabled the drover to guide his cattle safely underneath the railway line without having to wait for the level crossing to open, patience not necessarily being a virtue of a herd of cattle deprived of their natural habitat.

The Austin FX3 taxi, seen on the left, was *the* taxi for those brought up in Britain from the late forties until the mid-sixties. It became an iconic public service vehicle of the 'swinging sixties' and was first brought into service in 1948. The 'black cab' was a familiar sight in London and gradually was evident in other towns and cities across Britain. The FX3 was manufactured by the Austin Motor Company in association with Carbodies, who built the bodywork for each vehicle. After the FX3 came the introduction of the FX4 in 1958 and this model lasted in various forms until late 1997, when the first of the current TX series was introduced. The Bristol Lodekka was an equally iconic vehicle of the same period. It was manufactured between 1949 and 1968 by Bristol Commercial Vehicles and was a lowered-height double-decker bus, particularly suitable for cross-country routes with their occasional low bridges. The local bus company in the Wirral, Crosville, was a major user of the Lodekka. The majority were supplied with a Gardner 5 or 6 cylinder engine but others were produced with a Leyland engine or Bristol's own notably gruff-sounding engine. With their strong, powerful engines and well-chosen gear ratios they provided fast, reliable progress on any challenging cross-country route – remember, in those days A-roads rather than motorways were the main highways.

Before personal transport for all became the order of the day, travelling by bus to and from town or sometimes on longer journeys, was an exciting prospect for many children. Fifty years ago, when this picture was taken, buses had conductors who had shiny-peaked caps, leather money bags, ticket machines with a bell and a roll of tickets and swung, (sometimes) like monkeys from rail to pole and poll to rail as if in a dance. The joy of being allowed to travel upstairs on a bus was immense, dependent, usually on physical ability of the relative you were with and how tempted they had been at the local Co-op. On top, you could see forever, over fields, over walls, into bedrooms and other secret, illicit places. You were, unwittingly, a witness to some things that you didn't fully understand – but boy, was it exciting, an unexpected peek into an adult world of mystery and surprise.

NOW THEN!
Time for reflection

Each generation thinks of itself as 'modern' at every stage of life and yet we are all relics and mementos of our own history. As time goes by, we cling on to our more modish and fashionable behaviour and attitudes, sometimes with the hope that we can defy the passage of time, despite our constant creation of 'the past' and our own archaeology. In the main, we all enjoy looking back and remembering with affection things done, things achieved and comparing the context of our early lives with 'improvements' made (sometimes) in more recent times. Things often seem not to be as good as in the 'olden days', but most of the time we are not looking at a level playing field. Perhaps inevitably, many of our childhood memories, whatever our age now, are of endless summers and snow-filled winters, a sort of 'local to us' and historically appropriate version of Dylan Thomas's 'A Child's Christmas in Wales'.

But for all of us, time marches on, and as we get older and it seems strange that we find ourselves attempting to explain to our eleven-year-old god-daughter that there *was* life, of a sort, before computers, emphasising simultaneously our incredibly ancient origins.

During the last one hundred and twenty years, wartime experiences and memories have often defined generations, although in more recent times, with involvement in new conflicts, even this timeline has had to be re-defined.

Progress in radio, TV and other electronic development has outstripped most people's imagination and provided a sometimes obsessive and questionable way of 'stuffing' our days. Until the middle of the twentieth century, children had to use their imagination, inventiveness and creativity. The streets were filled with groups of youngsters of different ages pretending to be somebody, somewhere and something else. This was fun for most, freeing and gentle in its stimulation and engendered a relevant and satisfactory competitiveness conducive to learning.

Left and below: Outside, including in the playground, improvisation was the name of the game. You didn't need a ball for a game of football – a tightly bound bundle of rags or clothes would do, with discarded jackets or pullovers for goalposts. There were games that matched the seasons, such as conkers for example; those determined to win often used tricky and dishonest ways to convert the simple conker into a hard and unyielding boulder to cheat their way to success. Later in the year it was marbles, with wonderful 'glass beads' put to aggressive and destructive use in order to determine 'top dog'. There were also collecting activities, often involving cards with familiar faces, sometimes footballers or film stars. Playground games were often determined by gender, with the differences usually marked by the polarising of physical prowess and single-mindedness on the one hand and a softer camaraderie and togetherness on the other.

Change their clothes and maybe this photograph would also epitomise children of a similar age today. 'What can we do?', 'what can we get away with?' or 'what can we do that we're not allowed to do?' – the eternal challenges of a potentially naughty childhood. The challenges are all there on the faces and in the body language of these children; the pretty, enigmatic and carefully turned-out and only young lady, looking wistfully into the future and already deciding that there 'must be more to life than this'. The embarrassed disinterest and arrogance of the boys, pretending to ignore this beauty in their midst, presumably because they have not a clue as to how to change this impasse and status quo which inevitably interferes with relations between the sexes at this age. The fact that the young lady has got herself up onto the wall despite her more cumbersome clothing *and* that she has bagged the best position must certainly have added to the boys' discomfort: some things never change.

Above: In Victorian times, posed family and group photographs became very popular, even among the poorer sections of the population. In these days, fashion for boys tended to be a miniaturised approximation of their fathers wardrobe, including the cloth cap for working families. The girls, by contrast, were encouraged at an early age to wear 'pretty' and bright things, generally less sober than the outfits their mothers wore. Photographs such as this, taken in the early twentieth century, also subtly emphasise the closeness of communities and the acute smallness of their world. Without personal transport, apart from a bicycle or a horse, and public transport outside towns and cities limited to the railways, life was lived and learned within a mile of home; the back yard was their district, the street was their county, their town was a foreign country and the Empire was simply theirs! – but impossible to comprehend.

Above: As the relentless ambition towards personal transportation continued through the twentieth century, by the 1930s it was still a dream for the working class, a possibility for the more thrifty in the middle class and an inevitability for the upper class. The fascination of the motor car was already forcing itself into the lives of a few fortunate children. Model cars to fit a small child were in limited circulation by the middle of the 1930s. Some were quite sophisticated in their design and construction, usually manufactured by the more upmarket toy companies. Their antidote, of course, for the less affluent masses, was a more primitive 'soap box', usually built at home in the yard by dad and son, but with the advantage of light weight, a simply effective and replaceable build quality and, most importantly, greater speed.

Below right: Throughout the twentieth century, Royal events continued to be the focus of unfettered, nationwide celebration. This view of a street party from 1937 to celebrate the Jubilee of King George VI and Queen Elizabeth, has an added poignancy. Little did these children know that this would be one of the last days of celebration before the onset of hostilities in World War II. It is sad to contemplate that seven years after this happy and joyful photograph was taken, many of the older boys in the picture would be serving on the front line and maybe changing the lives of their families for ever. Typically, these boys want to be at the front of the picture, even if it means that they have to dance with each other! A photograph such as this captures the freedom and spontaneity of childhood innocence as set against the impending horror and finality of conflict.

Right: Towards the end of Queen Victoria's reign, at the turn of the twentieth century, women lived in a world of restriction and repression. They were not *all* unhappy *all* of the time but their lives were largely fashioned and ordered by men, if not husbands, then fathers. Male rules, male dominance, male control – of female lives. The First World War, or Great War as it was called, was suddenly upon the country, changing everyone's lives forever. With so many men rushing off to war, leaving girlfriends, wives and mothers behind, the order of life was disrupted and, over time, the minutiae of daily routines were increasingly dependent on women. Subjugation and subservience were not quickly forgotten but increasingly put to one side as new responsibilities were taken up, with a sensitivity and emotional response to the tougher things in life. Gender became an issue in the work place as remaining men looked on aghast as women pushed their way forward into traditional male roles, including those requiring substantial physical strength and effort. Women were soon to be seen at the heart of communities, taking a lead in ensuring that people were safe and cared for, that children continued to be educated and disruptions were kept to a minimum. Women also took on their expected roles, such as nurses and ambulance drivers, as well fulfilling their responsibilities as daughters, wives and mothers. At the beginning of World War I, women had little or no possibility of working near the front line, unless they were prepared and qualified to nurse. National and local charities contributed funds

and goods, such as bandages, basic food items, clothing and other daily necessities to a large number of War Hospital Depots which had been set up across the country. For women who had considered nursing as a wartime occupation these depots offered an alternative.

The empowerment of women during World War I carried them into a new era through the 1920s and 1930s. They had, to some extent, been liberated from the often oppressive rules left over from Victorian society. The men who returned from the war found, in many cases, a different woman waiting for them. The fashion, music and dances of the 1920s also gave women more choice, more confidence and the feeling that relationships with their men-folk, at last, included an element of sharing as opposed to endurance. As the 1930s slipped by, many found it impossible to contemplate further crisis in Europe, despite the looming on the horizon of a megalomaniac demagogue in the form of a small insignificant man destined to become the most evil dictator the world had known and at any cost. Women were more prepared for World War II, however, and men felt obliged to respect their abilities and potential by allowing them a greater share of responsibility in the war effort and in keeping the country ticking over. In 1940, as in this picture, ordinary yet committed teams of women went about their war work, looked after a house and family and probably did volunteer work as

well. The new-found confidence of women in all aspects of their personal lives, did not, however, adequately prepare them for the social and sexual pressures that tumbled towards their loneliness and isolation. Pressured by their boyfriends to move a relationship too rapidly past the bedroom door on the suggestion that it might be the last chance to 'have fun', many women found themselves alone with pregnancy, followed by a baby, often unwanted, as they fought the prejudices of their families as well as the enemy. The emotional extremes of life in World War II were almost too much to bear for some women.

The duties carried out by female members of the Royal Family during World War II, added to the notion that women's roles had moved on and they could, when necessary, deputise more than adequately for their male counterparts.

At the end of World War II, the continued stoicism of women was required in order for them to learn to live with the return of a 'man of the house' so very different to the one who had walked out of the front door months or years before, as well as 'making a meal' out of rationing and shortages for years to come. For some women, born in the twilight of the nineteenth century, their whole life had been a homage to conflict, altered values and unbelievable social change. Their experience and result persuaded the next generation to push on for even greater equality.

Above: From 1900 onwards, film and cinema stimulated the wildest dreams and desires of everybody they touched; romance, adventure, danger and excitement were served up in large dark rooms, firstly with music and later with voices, as technology caught up with the idea and pushed it to new horizons. In this picture from the 1940s, the influence of actors such as Errol Flynn is blatantly obvious in a game involving bows and arrows. His playing of Robin Hood against Olivia de Havilland as Maid Marian had a ground-breaking impact for some little boys, that remained with them into their teenage years (and in some cases even longer!). Having learned, by the age of six, how to buckle their belt, it was, after all, Errol Flynn who taught them how to 'buckle their swash' and 'get the girl'! Cinema has always had an influence on children's re-enactment and performance of stories and fables. Certainly children in the 1940s rarely complained about boredom or having 'nothing to do'. They simply grasped the nettle and worked out for themselves, using their imagination, what they could turn it into and they did it together – a sort of in-house approach to everyday life!

Right: In the 1950s, toys were still quite simple, for boys and girls. The only chips in sight were the ones sat on a plate next to the fish every Friday and enhanced with salt and vinegar - if you were lucky! In a society which still placed the emphasis on women as home makers and 'baby makers', toy companies were still making a lot of money from selling pretty little dolls to pretty little girls, banking on their softness and fondness for small, defenceless creatures in their own image. This wonderful picture, taken in 1950, shows two such little girls enjoying posing for a 'family' photograph, no doubt repeated twenty years later as the 'real thing'! Note the grittily determined, no-nonsense expression of the young lady at the back and the rather shyer, slightly myopic expression of the seated young lady with hair that, possibly, she has spent the rest of her life not being able 'to

do a thing with'! 'Out of the mouths of (female) babes and sucklings' came the maternal instinct, often honed through years of practice and monitored by an effective and unremitting body clock. And so it was ever thus...

Top right: For some, school days *were* happy days; the opportunity to be part of a team, to prepare for future adulthood by learning about ideas and theories that, when competently practised, could result in your being elected to run the country – or maybe not! Through the 1950s, classes in single-sex schools, continued to protect the idea that learning without obvious distraction was the only way to learn. The downside, of course, was the ease with which some boys slipped into an instinctive and damaging bullying role, with other doubters eventually linking in out of fear for their own well-being.

Right: Once upon a time, Monday was the traditional wash day for many. For working class families, the burden fell upon Mum. Her role as a housewife meant that the day was spent boiling clothes in a tub and then wringing them out through the mangle before pegging them out on the line in the back yard, or if you were *very* lucky, back garden. Before the days of sophisticated washing powders and rubber gloves, reddened hands were her

reward and there were still beds to be made, carpets to beat and lino to wash. Later, children needed feeding and the evening meal had to be ready and on the table when dad arrived home from work. It was hard work and there were few, if any, modern electrical appliances or 'white goods' to make the task of running the home any easier. Many working class families lived in terraced housing, some of it back to back, with outdoor 'lavvies', where you learned the skill of

whistling, with one foot jammed against the door in case someone else attempted to enter this small enclave of privacy. Many houses still had a tin bath that was dragged in from the yard and then filled with kettle after kettle of boiling water before family members took it in turn to soak themselves. This photograph, taken in the 1950s, shows a typical scene of what life was like in these circumstances; families and communities were close knit, sharing each other's joys and sorrows. It was quite common to lend a neighbour a helping hand in times of need. Friendships were often formed that lasted a lifetime.

Right: By the late 1950s, firmly turning our back on the gloom and shortages of wartime, the introduction and use of new materials led to the arrival of new ideas and new toys for children. This picture, taken around 1960, of a small child on a rocking horse, illustrates a modern interpretation of an age-old dream of many small children. From the days when horses were the only form of transport, little girls and boys

wanted to 'do what daddy did'. Wooden rocking horses have been created over a longer period than most other toys, probably for almost 200 years, and have provided a tangible link with life over the previous century. The popularity of films set in the Wild West in the 1950s probably assisted a minor renaissance in demand for toy horses.

From the 1960s onwards, toys have become more and more sophisticated, from electric models trains, accurate scale models of road vehicles of the day to that giant of practical and educational toys, Meccano and, of course, the ubiquitous and still vastly popular Lego. Over the last fifty years, more and more emphasis has been placed on the educational and learning value of toys to the extent that it is now not deemed reasonable to even refer to them as toys. The advent of simple and later more sophisticated electronic applications, largely from the rapidly expanding Far East, changed the world of toys into a more pressured and competitive environment for parents and children than ever before. Gone were the days when dad stood in his shed, cellar or back yard and fabricated out of a selection of useless left-overs, a wondrous, working and exciting replica, resembling, however vaguely, some daily artefact from the real world.

Above: With the massive increase in personal transport, road safety has become a major issue for all of us in our lifetime and has been written into the school curriculum since the middle of the twentieth century. At the beginning of this chapter, looking at the way we were, we see photographs of children playing games in the street: they also rode their bicycles on the carriageway with little danger to life or limb. With the steady increase in traffic in the 1930s, safety became an obvious and challenging issue and with statistics showing an alarming rise in accidents, the government of the day was obliged to take action. Driving tests were introduced: yes, up to this point you did not need a licence or take a test to be let loose on the road at ultimate speeds not too dissimilar from those attainable by a small saloon today – astonishing, or so it seems with hindsight. Belisha beacon crossings appeared in towns and cities and that well-known bestseller, The Highway Code, was formulated and published by His Majesty's Stationery Office.

After the Second World War, many local councils turned their attention to the safety and protection of children, who, at the time, lacked awareness of the dangers that existed in merely crossing the road or cycling to the shops. In this picture, taken in 1950, youngsters are given instruction on a model roadway system. Stop, look and listen were watchwords drummed into children together with instruction on how to use pedestrian crossings safely. Too many young people lost their lives through ignorance and, generally, the population were happy to see schemes, such as cycle proficiency, being promoted. In later years, we saw the Tufty Club, the Green Cross Code and, frighteningly, a fully permed Kevin Keegan advising us on why it was *not* a good idea to run out from behind parked cars! Sometimes, it all seemed a little light-hearted, but, as always, having fun whilst learning at least aided the retention of this information in the minds of children.

Bottom left: In this photograph, taken in 1960, we are reminded of how in childhood the world is divided into two, between those who love taking part in sport and those who hate it. Many of us looked forward to that afternoon period which included 'games', particularly in the summer, maybe to the sound of willow on leather and the chance to compete and play in a team; the chap on the right doesn't look too pleased – maybe that's because 'teacher' has asked him to carry the rounders bat and he is already worrying that he might have to play with the girls - NO WAY! From the well advanced garden greenery behind and the wearing of woolly tops, one must surmise that we are looking at a post summer holiday scene with the chance to impress and become part of the school team long gone. On the left of the picture, the games teacher's outfit of white top, skirt and plimsolls suggests that she believes it is still summer and will demand the same 100% effort from absolutely everyone. After an initial scramble on the field to find a place on the boundary – less stressful, less running – provided you could throw, we all accepted our lot and relaxed the afternoon away, just glad for once to be out of the classroom.

In the intervening years, many areas of sport have become very competitive, not least in some cases because of the 'pots of gold' at the end of the rainbow for those talented enough to find a place in professional sport. Sports, which in the 1950s were amateur in structure and operation, have more recently become professional, and, in some cases, highly rewarded financially. Similarly, the Olympic movement has now accepted the inclusion of all competitors, whether amateur or professional. On home territory, local councils under pressure to build more houses have been tempted into selling off acres of sports fields for construction, this coinciding with a generic deterioration of children's health through a relentless and on-going relationship with fast food. In contrast, fitness centres and activities have flourished through private initiatives for adults who, like their children, have become stereotypes for the couch potato.

So, the 'games period' in schools has changed somewhat from what we see in the photograph here, not least because of the sedentary pressures and pleasures most of us are now tempted to indulge in as well as the impact of outside forces. Massive improvements in health care and potential longevity for us all have also filtered down to become major factors in our younger lives – a sort of safety net of promise!

Above right: Ernest Evans was a fan of the legendary 1950s rocker Fats Domino and used his name as the inspiration to change his own name to Chubby Checker. His first big hit in Britain was in 1963 with 'Let's Twist Again', a follow-up to 'The

Twist', a record that, ironically, only became popular the following year. By 1963, as this couple attempted to keep their seams straight as they girated in the restricted confines of the 'front room' to the music from their Dansette record player, Chubby's star had already begun to wane. He switched to the limbo in an attempt to promote another dance form, but with limited success. However, re-issues of his twist records enjoyed a new popularity, particularly in the nineties, but sadly, only added to the cringe factor for those forced to watch as couples took to the floor, yet again, to the sound of 'Twist and Shout' or 'Peppermint Twist'. This was a craze that ensured the embarrassment of countless children at weddings, twenty-first celebrations and parties through the 1990s, as parents risked hernias and heart attacks and

every other ailment known to man, as they attempted to 'twist the night away', whilst their watching offspring felt afraid, very afraid!. 'Gosh Mum, you're so embarrassing!' or similar was heard with persistent regularity. But hang on there, it is my Mum after all – and so we remember these strange fashions and rituals with perhaps the affection they deserve!

In the end, we accept that the march of time continues to take us into new experiences, new rituals and, maybe, new horrors every day, all of which become part of our own rich and personal counterpane of human existence. We are reminded that 'life' is the REAL THING and not a rehearsal.

HAVE WHEELS, WILL TRAVEL
Moving on

By 1900, the railways had been plying their trade for over 60 years. Not that their introduction had been without issue. In 1830, landowners held a monopoly on much of the landscape, charging for anything that happened on it and for anything crossing it. When the horse and carriage routes demanded more sophisticated tracks to enable them to increase their speed across the landscape, Turnpike Trusts were established to facilitate the construction of early roadways or turnpikes and consisted, predominantly, of landowners, determined to retain their grasp on the purse of opportunity and profit. The turnpikes were welcomed as they often improved the quality of movement across the countryside for the landowner and his employees without his further personal investment.

The railways, however, were different. Firstly, whilst all landowners were not 'luddites', the thrusting and industrial challenge of the railways was largely beyond the experience and knowledge of the average 'countryman'. Secondly, the perceived disruption to the landscape was potentially massive as was the disturbance to livestock. Thirdly, the railways would almost certainly disrupt the role of the horse, certainly in rural society, again to the potential disadvantage of the landowner. Some landowners, particularly those who had become Members of Parliament, had eventually recognised the future of this new invention and saw the potential for an additional income stream. Initially, railway travel could only be afforded by the better off but as the impact of the railways increased and passenger numbers rose, so more people began to accept

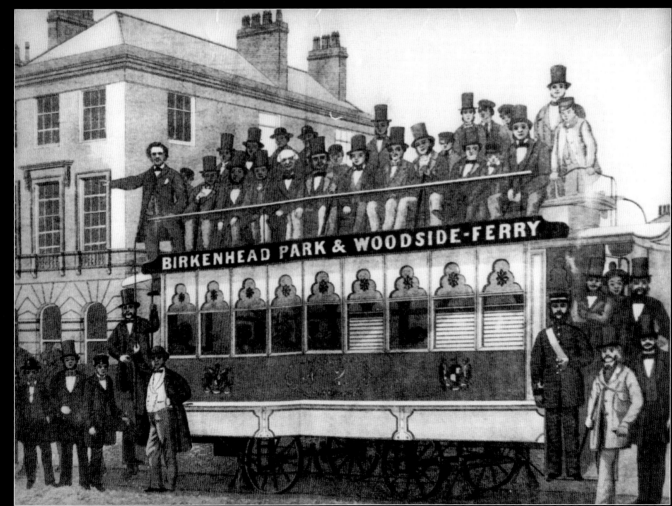

their place as a major contributor to travel and transport. By 1900, steam locomotives were criss-crossing the landscape in every direction, supported by a plethora of private railway companies keen to enjoy the success of a 'new' industry. These massive and romanticised 'Iron Horses' with their hissing, wheezing and rattling and their alluring combination of smells of smoke, oil and coal made a phenomenal contribution to industry over 120 years until their demise in the 1960s. When railways were moving people between town and city around the turn of the century, the only buses available were horse-drawn and they were few and far between. Only when motor buses came on the scene around 1904 did public transport become available for large sections of the population. Early buses were essentially horse-drawn carriages with an engine stuck on the front and enjoying the same wooden wheels and primitive cart suspension and an abominable ride quality. In the absence of personal transport for most of us, buses remained the backbone of travel provision for another 50 years.Cars were available to the upper classes from the turn of the century, barely there for the middle classes from the 1930s and only widely accessed by the working classes from 1960s onwards, from whence we descended into the grid-lock we 'enjoy' on a daily basis today, as ownership became part of a fashion and an expectation that no-one could be denied.

Left: August 30, 1860 was a red letter day, not just for Birkenhead, but for the whole of Europe. This day saw the introduction of the first street tramway in Europe, running from Woodside to Birkenhead Park. The gentleman on the top deck of the tram, to the left, pointing down the street, is George Francis Train, an American who had brought this early horse-drawn tram system from America. He was rumoured to be the real-life model on whom the celebrated author Jules Verne based his hero of 'Around the World in Eighty Days', Phileas Fogg. Train imported the tramcars in sections from America and they were reconstructed by a local coachbuilder. On February 4, 1900, the first electric tramway was introduced on the New Ferry route. After the innovation to bring trams to Birkenhead it is strange that the town was one of the first to retire trams from its streets, in July, 1937.

Left: Woodside remained a busy transport 'interchange' for many years, bringing people into the town centre from the adjacent ferry terminal. This picture taken in 1929 shows a collection of trams waiting for a turn of duty, as did similar collections of buses from 1937 onwards.

Below: Whilst the Mersey Railway Tunnel was opened as early as 1886, it was forty years later before it was deemed necessary to consider creating a road tunnel under the river.

In this photograph, taken on the Cheshire side of the River Mersey on March 10th, 1926, we see Sir Archibald Salvidge, First Chairman of the Mersey Tunnel Joint Committee, commencing excavations on the original tunnel shaft at Morpeth Dock, Shore Road, by 'raising the first sett'. This first road tunnel, running from Liverpool to Birkenhead, the Queensway Tunnel, opened to traffic in 1934 and it was another 37 years before a second road tunnel, the Kingsway Tunnel, running from Liverpool to Wallasey, opened to traffic.

For many people in the 1920s, their only direct experience of road travel was an occasional trip or outing in a charabanc, an open vehicle with rows of transverse seats or benches. Personal transport at this time, for most people apart from the wealthy, consisted of a bicycle or a horse if you were lucky. The philanthropic approach of some employers towards their employees included the provision of an annual works outing to the races, some other relatively local event, or the seaside: preferably not too far, as the wheels were wooden and the suspension, for what it was, from something just a tiny bit more ambitious than a farmer's horse-drawn cart – comfort was not included at any price.

It is interesting to note that the chassis for these vehicles was a simple ladder frame for a primitive flat-bed lorry. It was no coincidence that the origin of many coach companies of later times was in early haulage companies at the start of the century. From the twenties, early flat-bed lorries were often used for local deliveries during the week with the flat-bed unbolted at the weekend and a simple boat-shaped charabanc body attached, with its rows of seats, ready for an exciting day out with you and your colleagues.

The Harding's charas in the picture are about to embark on a police and tradesmen's outing, maybe to the gentle, undulating and empty Cheshire countryside, the historic delights of nearby Chester, or even, to wet their feet and

their whistles on the seafront at Rhyl, on the nearby North Wales coast! In the other photograph, an early chara belonging to the well-known Crosville Company is seen, in 1920, on the annual Kingsmead School trip to Moel Famau in North Wales. One can only imagine the excitement that this outing presented for young people of the school, not only climbing a mountain, but a motorised journey, there and back!

Crosville, the name being an amalgamation of the two founders' names, George CROSland Taylor and Georges de VILLE, was created in 1906 with the intention of producing motor cars. However, buses and the services they provided in the region remained the core of the business until the company disappeared after de-regulation in the 1980s.

Above: Seacombe was already a thriving shipbuilding centre in the 1800s and ferries have for a long time, plied their journeys out of the Seacombe Ferry Terminal. By the 1920s, when this photograph was taken, 32 million passengers per year were using the Seacombe ferry. From the picture, we can surmise that a major event is about to take place; the body language and dress of the people suggest something 'special' is about to happen. Many have come in their own private cars, unusual so early in the century and suggestive of an event that might appeal to the better off. Ferries across the Mersey have always taken the headlines, musical or otherwise, but the ferry from Seacombe to Birkenhead, permission for which was granted by the Earl of Chester, probably in the fifteenth or sixteenth century, was an original and major development in the region.

Top right: Coach travel in the 1950s had certainly moved on from the crudely constructed 'charas' of the 1920s and, whilst still based on lorry chassis, they had begun to incorporate 'proper' suspension more appropriate to the support of bottoms than boxes! The model on the left of this photograph, of two Harding's coaches taken in the 1950s, looks like an AEC Regent based single-decker, often used on urban and rural bus routes with low bridges. The vehicle on the right was a very distinctive looking coachbuilt vehicle based on a Leyland Comet lorry.

But the camel! Whilst New Brighton had a well-loved beach it could not be mistaken for a desert. Hardings, who have now been in the business of moving happy families around the country in a variety of vehicles for over a hundred years, obviously decided that the suspension was now good enough to demonstrate these two extremes of travel as a positive part of their marketing campaign!

Below: Starting out as a small engineering and blacksmith business in the late nineteenth century, Leyland produced their first bus in 1899 and for the rest of the twentieth century the name was synonymous with vehicle production. This picture, taken at Arrowe Park roundabout in 1955, shows a Leyland Titan PD2/12, number 256, part of a second batch of Leyland PD2's delivered to the Corporation. As more people explored the possibility of owning their own personal transport, the level of bus passengers declined and transport strategies had to be re-defined. With a boost in house building in the sixties, the trend was reversed in some areas but routes had to be re-organised to accommodate these demographic changes.

Bottom, this page: This view shows a building owned by W. Watson and Company, in Hamilton Street, Birkenhead, and used in 1938 to store an impressive selection of vehicles hoping for customers. Although at this late stage there were some who still did not believe that the threat of a major war would materialise, we can imagine that some of these vehicles failed to find customers. Mothballing them until the end of the conflict six years later *was* possible, not least because it was almost 1950 before manufacturers had the opportunity to re-group, replacing wartime production lines with the pre-war dies until they could afford to create new designs. So, new cars produced in the first years after the war were essentially identical to those made in 1938 – but at least they were new.

Bottom right, facing page: This wonderful photograph taken in April, 1930, at Birkenhead Woodside, epitomises steam travel; you can almost detect the smells and hear the sounds by looking at such a picture. The engine is No 5365 George V Racehorse from GWR's Toplight stock. Having said that, you can conclude that the two railwaymen could not have imagined how we would get 'all steamed up' 50 years or more later, over these behemoths of the track, romanticising their rumble and their clackety-clack and happily choking on a mixture of oil, coal and steam. It is easy to see how the rhythmic chant of those huge wheels along the track provided the inspiration for 'Coronation Scot', the tune that heralded the popular radio detective adventures of Paul Temple – do you remember?

In this view of the West Kirby junction, we can see in the centre the station building, erected in 1896, which in more recent times was the terminus for the Merseyrail Wirral Line. In 1937, when this photograph was taken, the railways were of massive importance in their ability to shift freight around the country. Long distance lorry traffic had not really been devdeloped and would be kept waiting until the advent of the motorways thirty years later.

Left: The ubiquitous 2-6-4 tank engine, pulling a short goods train on the Hooton to West Kirby line, typifies branch line activity at the end of the fifties and the beginning of the sixties: single, overgrown track, half-full wagons, little investment and a sense that this couldn't go on much longer. It didn't.

Above: The beginning of the 1960s saw the true dawn of the motorway age and the era of personal transport for all. This massive and fundamental swing in favour of all aspects of road use was a blind and maniacal act as short-sighted and dangerous as you could possibly imagine. Yes, with hindsight we can all complain about the errors of the past, but this rejection of the railways had consequences way beyond any transport consideration and shunted a great chunk of social history into the sidings to rust and rot away with the insistence of successive governments that we should forget and move on. Railways became an integral part of life on the Wirral Peninsular from the middle of the nineteenth century onwards. The railway arrived at Hoylake in 1866, linking it directly with the docks station on the other side of the peninsular. An extension to West Kirby was completed in 1879, enabling those who worked in Birkenhead and Liverpool to enjoy the possibility of living in rural communities surrounded by green fields and woodland. The prosperity of the whole peninsular was positively affected by the expansion of the railways enabling visitors to consider it as a different and accessible destination for a holiday. By the end of the 1950s, many could see the beginning of a slow slide into disuse and dereliction for the railways and by 1962 the junction at West Kirby was deemed unnecessary and superfluous.

This photograph, taken on May 7 1962, shows the last freight train on its way out of West Kirby station, pulled by an LMS 2-6-4 tank engine, number 42229, on its final journey to Hooton, axed with great force and immediacy by a certain Dr. Beeching. As part of a plan to develop the railways, or so we were told, the network was butchered beyond repair and whole communities in rural areas across Britain woke up, from one day to the next, to find themselves dramatically cut off and isolated, not to mention inconvenienced. Even the body language of the children in the picture, sitting on a redundant luggage cart, suggests a sadness in defeat, not in a battle fought and lost but more in a devious and disguised thrust from a weapon out of the blue.

SHOP-PORTUNITIES!

Retail therapy

A hundred years ago, shopping was for necessities and this was reflected in the type of shops that existed in town and city centres. You went shopping if you needed something, not just because you wanted it; life in those days had other priorities more directly related to family and survival. Fortunately, in the midst of our ongoing obsession with large, covered, out-of-town shopping centres, we manage to recall their predecessors, the markets.

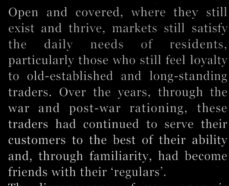

Open and covered, where they still exist and thrive, markets still satisfy the daily needs of residents, particularly those who still feel loyalty to old-established and long-standing traders. Over the years, through the war and post-war rationing, these traders had continued to serve their customers to the best of their ability and, through familiarity, had become friends with their 'regulars'.

The disappearance of many open-air markets coincided with the increasing spread of supermarkets and changes in shopping patterns which now included personal transport and the imposed idea of 'one-stop shopping'. For some shopping has become an 'obsession', for others no longer a 'pleasure' and, today, for many, something that does not even involve a 'shop'.

Left: Today, many of us are obsessed by shoes, but it is difficult for us, literally, to put ourselves 'in the shoes' of our ancestors a hundred years ago. Fulfilling the need was ALL that mattered to most people and two pairs of shoes were all that most people owned, one for work and one for best and the most important consideration when buying shoes was that they would last. To own and use a pair of

shoes for less than ten years was an extravagance and cobblers were not short of trade.

Retail shops in 1900 were generally individual businesses, run by a local family. Duckworth's shoe shop, in Birkenhead, seen here in the early years of the twentieth century, would base its reputation on quality of construction and consequently longevity. As the century progressed, Britain developed a reputation for producing good quality shoes and centres such as Northampton became synonymous with the manufacture and marketing of footwear. After the 1970s, the chains of shoe shops we had become used to on every high street across the country began to phase out UK manufactured shoes in favour of cheaper, mass produced shoes, mainly from the Far East, as British labour costs outstripped the potential for even a glimmer of a profit margin for the domestic industry.

Above: This picture, taken at the turn of the twentieth century, shows the Market Square, adjacent to the rear of the Market Hall on the right of the picture. Again we can see how a lack of any motorised traffic left town centre squares relatively open and pleasant.

Birkenhead Market, built in 1845, was the first market hall to be constructed with a glass and wrought iron roof, a style that was to become increasingly popular. The market was founded in 1835 on the site of Birkenhead Town Hall, between Chester Street and Hamilton Street, moving to a

nearby location ten years later. Michael Marks, of Marks & Spencer, opened one of his first seven 'Penny Bazaar' stalls on this site in 1880.

The photographs left and below, taken in roughly the same period, show the covered storage area for produce and the vehicles used for transporting goods, parked in lines, with some brave outside stall-holders arranged against the railings in the background. The photograph, bottom left, provides a good indication of how the inside of the Market Hall looked, butchers appearing prominent along the left-hand wall. As today, markets have always been perceived as the purveyors of the best value and a sound mixture of businesses provided an early version of modern supermarket one-stop shopping philosophy. Even now market stalls provide a first stepping stone into business for many people, with lower overheads and a ready, well-established clientele. In more recent times, in 1969 and 1974, fires in the market forced a move to a new site adjacent to the Grange Shopping Precinct. Interesting that, as we write in 2009, in the middle of a severe, 'credit crunch', it is the markets that are enjoying increasing trade in contrast to almost every other kind of business.

FUN AND GAMES

relax and enjoy

Victorian times ensured that fun and games were enforced upon and 'enjoyed' almost exclusively by children and promoted to them as something 'you will grow out of'. Morality, obedience and principles were exercised and endured remorselessly. Enjoyment as *we* know it, only came later! Look at a picture of the seaside anywhere in Britain at the turn of the twentieth century and you are struck by the long black clothing (usually made of wool) – combine this thought with sand and its irritative qualities and somehow the seaside does not seem as attractive a place to be as today with our more relaxed and precocious approach to clothing – or lack of it. Over the last century, children did play together, spontaneously and using their creativity and imagination, learning to 'make do' without the perfect ingredients for every game. The playground, either school or public, launched millions of ideas and fantasies, some developed, some never – but at least they gave it a go.

Public leisure amenities have been around for a long time. The provision of public open spaces became popular at the end of the nineteenth century, particularly in urban industrial environments where the poorly housed workforce did not always have the opportunity to escape to the countryside in some shape or form. Providing open parks on the edge of towns, served by cheap public transport, often cooled the resentment of the more challenging workers. Natural and healthy existing environments could also be used to entice visitors from further afield – we now

call them tourists. The more the merrier thought the local council and with the appropriate mix of trees, grass, bandstands, ice cream parlours and deckchairs, so was created your instant resort – New Brighton, for example.

Above: By the third quarter of the nineteenth century, winter sport in Britain was essentially divided between soccer and rugby, although the latter had not yet firmed up into the codes that we recognise today. However, in 1871, a meeting took place which effectively presaged the future of rugby with its two disciplines, league and union. Whilst it is still, to this day, argued as to the real origin of the name 'rugby', sceptics being unwilling to accept the potentially 'apocryphal' story of William Webb Ellis's spontaneous decision in 1823 to ignore existing rules of the game, in a match played at Rugby School. There is little, on record, of the history of Birkenhead Rugby League Club, but they still appeared in a league table around 1904. This picture of the club's team was taken in 1898.

Top right: To this day, in smaller communities across the country, cricket is what you play in the summer, sometimes competitively, sometimes just for fun. The frisson created by the smell of new-mown grass, the sound of willow striking leather and the spontaneous and hopeful cry of 'how's that' coinciding with the clatter of falling wickets can be addictive for some, as a

player or as a spectator. Although cricket is a different game today with the impact of commercialism and celebrity hype, the essence and appeal remains the same for most of us. This picture, taken in the Wirral in the 1920s, could just as well have been taken yesterday!

Below: Tranmere Rovers Football Club was formed from two local cricket clubs and played its first match in 1886. Living in the shadow of the two big Merseyside clubs, Liverpool and Everton, Tranmere have had their high points connected by periods of floating up and down the Football League, but have always

managed to attract some well-known names. Dixie Dean, Pat Nevin, Steve Coppell, Steve Davies, John Aldridge and Jason Koumas have all played for Tranmere and former England player, Tommy Lawton, played for the club during World War II. The photograph shows the 1978-79 team, with a recent manager, Ronnie Moore, eighth from the left, and commentator Ray Stubbs second from the right, both on the back row. The club is currently celebrating its 125th year, having moved into the Prenton Park Stadium in 1912. In recent times, former England player John Barnes, as manager, with former player, Jason McAteer, as his assistant have been and gone

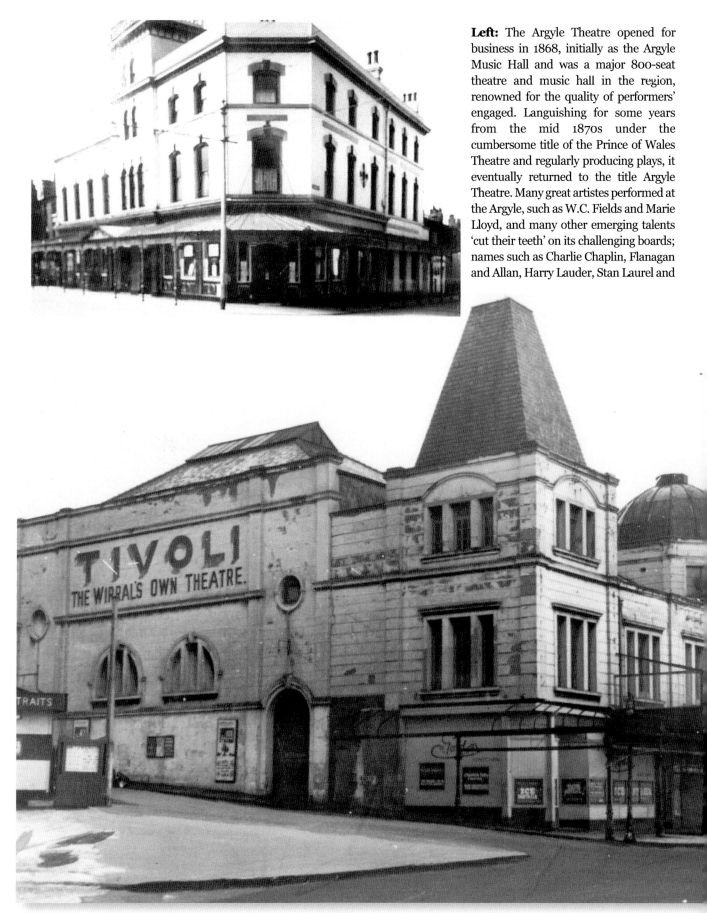

Left: The Argyle Theatre opened for business in 1868, initially as the Argyle Music Hall and was a major 800-seat theatre and music hall in the region, renowned for the quality of performers' engaged. Languishing for some years from the mid 1870s under the cumbersome title of the Prince of Wales Theatre and regularly producing plays, it eventually returned to the title Argyle Theatre. Many great artistes performed at the Argyle, such as W.C. Fields and Marie Lloyd, and many other emerging talents 'cut their teeth' on its challenging boards; names such as Charlie Chaplin, Flanagan and Allan, Harry Lauder, Stan Laurel and

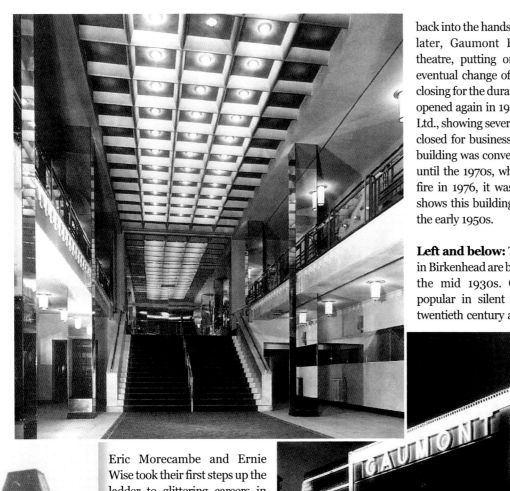

back into the hands of Fred Ross in 1926. Two years later, Gaumont British Company bought the theatre, putting on films and shows, which an eventual change of name to the New Tivoli. After closing for the duration of World War II, the theatre opened again in 1945, owned by Lean Productions Ltd., showing several seasons of plays until it finally closed for business in 1955. Many years later, the building was converted into an amusement arcade until the 1970s, when it was closed down. After a fire in 1976, it was demolished. This photograph shows this building in its final theatrical heyday in the early 1950s.

Left and below: The Gaumont and Ritz Cinemas in Birkenhead are both seen here in their heydays in the mid 1930s. Cinema had already become popular in silent form at the beginning of the twentieth century and as technology catapulted its

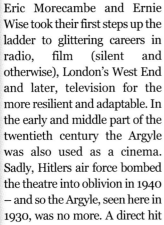

Eric Morecambe and Ernie Wise took their first steps up the ladder to glittering careers in radio, film (silent and otherwise), London's West End and later, television for the more resilient and adaptable. In the early and middle part of the twentieth century the Argyle was also used as a cinema. Sadly, Hitlers air force bombed the theatre into oblivion in 1940 – and so the Argyle, seen here in 1930, was no more. A direct hit left the shell of the building, unusable but it was not demolished for another thirty-three years.

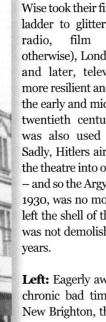

Left: Eagerly awaited, but with unwittingly chronic bad timing, the Tivoli Theatre in New Brighton, the buzzing and vibrant and convenient resort for Merseysiders, opened its doors on April 6, 1914, with the famous entertainer, Lilly Langtry, at the top of the bill. For the next nine years, the theatre was managed by Fred Ross who was responsible for promoting the Tower Ballroom. After two further changes of ownership, the theatre fell

volume and quality into availability for all, so with the onset of sound and the spoken word and the later introduction of colour, this popular medium first occupied the population through the tougher moments of the century and later prepared it for the advent of 'pictures on a box' in their own homes; when we accede to our obsession and pre-occupation with all aspects of television today, it is easy to forget these early years of the 'magic lantern'. The architectural obsessions of the 1920s and 1930s embraced cinema buildings in a big way, bringing Art Deco, in particular, to 'a cinema near you'! The Odeon style of design was easily recognised but the lesser remarked upon Gaumont style was similar to Burtons in terms of its frontage. Many former Odeon still survive as Bingo halls and both styles, where they remain, have been embraced by fast food outlets across the country.

Above: There's a big difference between a trip to the seaside in 1900 and a hundred years later in 2000. Certainly, in 1900, everybody was inclined to cover themselves up, usually with something black and woolly. A century later, it seemed more like a competition as to how much you could uncover and catch people's eye with!

Beach huts and windbreaks were very common, and, at some resorts, bathing vans were the norm, allowing you the privacy to descend in your woolly one-piece directly into the water, so avoiding prying eyes until you were neck deep in the ocean. Behind closed curtains, the Victorians were probably as licentious as anyone else, but in public arenas prudity, usually, held out. This picture of the New Brighton beach in 1900 shows the unusual sight of a fairground, presumably far enough away from the tidal waters of the Irish Sea. The essential elements of fairgrounds in this era, namely swings and roundabouts, are much in evidence, demonstrating a determination to offer something for all ages. For the first half of the twentieth century, *all* resorts were for familis simply because families did things together.

Bottom left: Sea, sun and sand, that elusive yet winning combination that has forever been sought out by the British as the prime constituent for a successful holiday, is epitomised here in New Brighton in 1949. The accessibility of New Brighton was a major factor for the slaves of industry and commerce in Birkenhead and Liverpool. This young lady has possibly finished her working day and hot-footed her way to her regular, if not exclusive, spot overlooking the river estuary, for a couple of hours of late afternoon warmth. New Brighton attracted a varied clientele but was probably best known for facilities associated with a more mature clientele and comfortable seating! For relative youngsters, a quiet spot in the sun was often enough.

Below: This picture of Wallasey Beach at New Brighton, taken in 1933, shows the resort at the height of its popularity, serving the region's population as an accessible seaside venue with all the amenities expected at the time. By the 1930s, most visitors had moved away from the 'Victorian' tendency to wear black to everything, including the beach, and wool was no longer always the material of choice – sand and wool? No thank you! By 1933, the woolly looks had been replaced by the odd splash of grey or beige and children began to bare their legs and Dad rolled up his sleeves, occasionally, whilst Mum fretted about all and everything and barely had time to enjoy the day. For Mum, with children to mind, the Tower Ballroom of her courting days was sadly now out of bounds and the roller coaster in the background was just a little too exciting.

Above: A promenade in 1900 was intended for just that, the opportunity to promenade and see and be seen. Bicycles were the chosen transport of the day. With their heavy long skirts even ladies' bicycles were not the easiest things to ride but the effort was well worth the freedom they provided and the opportunity they gave young women to push out the parameters of their lives. The gentle bobbing of the sailing craft in the shore area added to the genteel and relaxing scene for the residents of Hoylake, whilst the steam powered merchant vessels on the horizon reminded visitors of the industry and trade they had left behind for the day.

Right: Take your small child on the beach and sand would continue to eminate from every nook, cranny, fold and orifice for a fortnight – but it was worth it for the laughter and amazement on your child's face as he or she, or both, thrilled to the scratchy, damp touch of this alien substance. The 'more sensible' mums would, of course, not countenance the gentle swerve required at the end of the Promenade to bring them onto the beach itself. Common sense, previous experience or possibly a lack of time, or all three, dictated a pavement passage with merely a view of others enjoying themselves – but without the mess at the end of it.

In this picture of the Promenade at Hoylake, taken at the turn of the twentieth century, it is clear that for ladies that summer straw boaters were 'the thing'.

Below: Lifeboats were stationed on or near the beach for very obvious reasons. The speed with which they could hit the water was critical. Here at Hoylake at the turn of the century, a crowd has gathered at the possibility of seeing the lifeboat being hauled down the beach and into the water. Young boys abound, as they always did, thinking maybe that manning the lifeboat was something they would try later on — and often did, because most lifeboats utilised volunteers from the local community.

Hoylake Swimming Pool was a great place to spend a sunny afternoon in the 1930s. Competition from other activities was limited and on a sunny summer afternoon, the outdoors, a patch of water and a group of friends was all you needed. By 1931, when this photograph was taken, the traumas and tragedies of the

Great War had faded into a distant memory and life assumed a normality and brighter colour than before. The persistent greys and blacks of the Victorian era had almost disappeared, at least for those under the age of forty, and the later gloom and dread of another war in Europe had not yet clouded our skies.

Right: This picture of Holiday Camp A at Moreton, taken in the early part of the twentieth century, provides a view of 'sheds' set in an unloved and rather unpromising landscape. Yet, at the time, it possibly satisfied the expectations of those who chose to holiday there. Your own place for a week, with an outdoor space bigger than your back yard, if you had one and air cleaner than that of your usual industrial environment -was a big attraction.

Left: Most seaside'resorts looked for unusual and original ways for entertaining visiting families to ensure their swift return. Offering an attraction which they could not find nearer home was the key. The , and a moderately used roadway alongside, provided the opportunity in New Brighton to construct a miniature railway, much to the excitement of visiting small children.

When this photograph was taken in 1951, the resort was entering its last decade of viability. As the fifties gathered pace, so did the alternative opportunities for trying something different and the increase in car ownership, fuelled by a post-war economy that slowly but surely was dragging itself away from the restrictions of the 1940s, gave more people the chance to look further afield.

The smallness of these miniature trains was the key to their success; children could better relate to the child-sized scale of the operation, almost as if, at last, someone had realised that children *are* smaller. Able to get closer to the action than with their full-sized counterparts, groups of small boys, as here, could almost minutely examine the workings of these little locomotives. For the driver, things were a bit trickier. As a full-sized adult, the struggle to manipulate each part of this miniature technical marvel was on-going and challenging, not least because, generally there would be no room for a fireman as well. This made it very important for the right hand to be absolutely sure as to what the left hand was doing. No doubt the joy of

unwinding his body back to full size at the end of a working day was equalled only by the happiness he could witness on the faces of visiting children. For the residents of the Liverpool side of the Mersey, New Brighton was a convenient and short crossing by ferry, just visible in this photograph at the end of the pier in the background. A year after these crowds thronged along the front at New Brighton, the first ever package flight took off from Liverpool Airport for the South of France and visitor numbers began a steady decline.

Above: As a destination for Third Age participants, New Brighton was still convenient for a day out. If we look closely at this photograph taken in 1961, we can discern the average age of deck-chaired visitors to be somewhere between 55 and 75. A sunny day chatting to old friends and acquaintances on the end of a pier with catering to hand and the river lapping gently beneath could still, for some, transport you away from the cares and mundanity of a normal day and provide a change which was often as good as a rest. Memories of childhood spent on this same chunk of pier, with the then attendant Punch and Judy, candy floss, ice creams and slot machines were enough to fuel this glimpse of the past. If you wanted a little exercise, a gentle stroll towards the Tower Ballroom and Theatre or a tasty peek into the delights of the Avondale Cafe would sate your appetite, until you arrived home for a late high tea, armed with a new and updated pack of memories with which to deal at a future date.

was good and something to look forward to. In reality, this could turn into abject fear at the thought of being asked to balance on the top of a living, moving and unpredictable creature. Donkeys were chosen as the four-legged transport of choice because of their predictably; the problem is that when they are unpredictable they are really unpredictable! Screams and tantrums permitting, we endured our short, bumbling and, frankly, rather unexciting sashay across fifty yards of sand and back. The point being that if we didn't experience this confrontation between child and beast we would scream ourselves hoarse

Above: For children, the seaside has for long provided a gold rush of different activities once a year or more. Depending on your age, different levels of excitement were engendered simply by the mention of buckets and spades, ice cream, crazy golf, shove ha'penny and donkeys.

The reality, on arrival at our beach of choice, was to frantically search for a piece of sand to call our own: this took time until it dawned on us that we would not be able to find a spot equidistant from the sea, the toilets, the ice creams and the donkeys. If we were very small, the idea of a ride on a donkey

for the rest of the day; why? – well, because this was what going to the seaside was all about. This photograph was taken on New Brighton beach in 1971, just one more season away from the closure of the Pier for good. It was eventually demolished in 1978.

Below: Arrowe Park, situated between Woodchurch and Thingwall, was once the estate of John Shaw, a Liverpool warehouse owner, who like many other Liverpool businessmen in the heyday of the Industrial Revolution,

sought out the relative peace and quiet and the open spaces of the rural Wirral Peninsular. He built Arrowe Hall in 1835 and developed a fine estate with landscaped grounds. In 1928, the park was sold to Birkenhead Corporation for public use. In this picture of the playground in the park, taken in 1960, the importance of outdoor areas for informal recreation is emphasised by the enormous number of children having fun together. Before the electronic era in which we now find ourselves, outdoor play was normal for most children, and even now, playing in the park still has a place in the lives of many families. Numerous nearby residents will no doubt have enjoyed this park for generations.

Above: The intensely compromised quality of urban industrial life in the early part of the nineteenth century posed a dilemma for many local authorities. Health issues, poor housing, low pay, inadequate sanitation and other issues eventually persuaded some local authorities to create accessible and local environments for ordinary people to experience landscaped open spaces, away from the smells, noise and pace of industry. Somewhere for families, living in tightly packed terraced housing with only a backyard for outdoor space, to relax and spend time together.

The immediate impact of this strategy can be seen on the faces and in the body language of the mums and children in this hazy study in light and shade, taken in Birkenhead Park in 1950. The local authority was a pioneer in the creation of a local municipal park in 1847. A 125-acre stretch of relatively useless land, between Claughton and the town centre, provided the great landscape architect, Sir Joseph Paxton, with a tricky yet promising canvas upon which to lay out a varied, exciting and enduring landscape in which local people could enjoy and experience a totally different aspect of life. The presence of so much water in the original landscape inspired in Paxton the imaginative creation of two substantial lakes with islands and mounds and vistas created from the resultant excavations, providing direction and ideas that were later mirrored in the somewhat more famous Central Park, in New York. For more than 150 years, the park has merited its place as an integral part of Birkenhead life.

A HARD DAY'S GRAFT

working life

One hundred years ago, life was substantially different to what it is today, not least in the 'world of work'. Things have changed radically for many of us as 'needs' have been replaced by 'desires'. Today, the pace of daily life is staggering and, for some of us, quite tough to keep up with. Choices, or lack of them, determined what we did or what we didn't or couldn't do. If we only had a horse, a bicycle or our own two feet as a means of moving around, we were limited to how far away from home we could work. Such basic considerations were common at a time when many people spent their whole lives within a mile or two of their front door. Families and a 'social life' could substantially influence your type and place of work; you could maybe find work where your brother or sister worked or maybe your Dad's best mate knew somebody who was looking for a strong, young lad like you to learn his trade.

The changing nature of the work place in your area, would sometimes offer new opportunities and new hope. If you lived near a busy river, you might have spent some time 'messing about in boats' and thereby gained skills to apply for certain jobs working on or near the water. Living in an area where a variety of opportunities arose as a result of entrepreneurial and visionary activity of individual business men and women also had an impact on the continued success of this area; the Wirral is, perhaps, a good example of this as, despite being dismissed as a backwater in earlier times, the region embraced, after the beginning of the Industrial Revolution, a committed and considered approach to new technology and world-wide opportunities for trade.

Below: At the beginning of the twentieth century, women's role in society was quite specific, controlled and without

choice. As the world staggered up to the gunshot that triggered the conflict and madness that evolved into the First World War, women were still entrenched in domestic and maternal activity with limited reference to work, politics and their implications. With tens of thousands of men swiftly despatched to engage with the King's cousin, Kaiser Wilhelm II, women found themselves at the sharp end in every community, learning to take charge, manage and make decisions. The task of maintaining the momentum on the home front presented a massive challenge to the female population, but they rose like a phoenix to maintain sanity and order with unquenchable fire and spirit.

Factories recruited women for almost every task and often, even where physical and strength requirements meant a revised way of doing things. The impetus of this wholesale takeover of work which had previously been completed by men was fuelled, of course, by the activities of the Suffragette Movement. The workers pictured here, in the 1920s, and many others, took full responsibility in every role presented to them, whether it was in weaving, engineering or driving heavy goods vehicles. Many took on volunteer work during the war and remained in industry at the end of hostilities, not always through necessity but sometimes through choice. Having excelled at creating a list of priorities

and demonstrated the ability to make the best decisions, women, understandably, wanted more from life than checking the requirements of a shopping list for the family or just agonising over whether to do the ironing before the cleaning. Between the wars, many men found it more than difficult to accept this new involvement by women, their desire to be involved in all aspects of family life and their refusal to be 'under the control' of their men folk. By the time World War II was on the horizon, women were already geared up for an even greater input into anything and everything, their appetite whetted, here was a chance to push out the boundaries even further.

Above: The opening by King George V and Queen Mary in 1934 of the new and grand Central Library in Borough Road, Birkenhead, certainly gave these two librarians something to smile about. The opportunity to work in a spacious, state-of-the-art building, handling books and archives and helping local people access the information of their choice must have seemed a relative luxury to many. Even the lender, sat at the table, has a contented and wistful look on her face. Today, things have surely changed, but thankfully, the building still provides a cool and spacious opportunity to explore the strange, obscured, protected and unknown.

Left: As the twentieth century rolled out, women increasingly found opportunities to work in factory environments, often, it must be said, completing tedious and repetitive tasks. The boredom was sometimes relieved by the joys of working in groups together with other women and girls of a similar age.

From the setting up of the railway network across the Wirral Peninsular in the mid – 1800s, connecting commuters quickly to Liverpool and its substantial industrial enterprise, a daily flow of willing women workers made the journey to factories such as Meccano in Binns Road, seen here in the 1940s. Meccano had been established in 1908, by Frank Hornby. It created and manufactured a series of toys which dominated the market from the 1920s to the 1950s, such as Hornby Model Railways, Dinky Toys and, of course, the famous metal building kits which gave the company its name. Following financial difficulties in the 1960s, the Meccano company was taken over by Lines Brothers, a well-known company trading under the name of Tri-ang. The idea of a team of women producing 'toys for boys' on a sleepless branch line creates an interesting frisson; but create they did for what became a world market.

Below: A genderised view of the workplace remained until World War II. During the war attitudes began to change as more women were allowed to take an active role in the armed forces. Yet again, women took the place of men in an even wider variety of jobs, simply on the basis that there was no alternative. There had still been, prior to hostilities, clearly defined areas of work deemed appropriate for women and other areas more typically fulfilled by men. The experience of women during the war doing unfamiliar and challenging work had an empowering effect. However, although 7.2 million women were in work during the war, this figure quickly dropped by over 20% by summer 1946. As this photograph taken in 1950 shows, some precedents were harder to break; the telephone operator was invariably a woman, whilst the person delivering the post was invariably a man. It took many more years for these stereotypes to change.

Above: After the makeshift scenario during World War II, local authorities made a conscious decision to upgrade their fire service activity, providing the latest appliances to deal with a rapidly changing townscape. In 1952, Birkenhead Fire Brigade took delivery of the hand-built Merryweather Thunderbird seen here, which was one of only three produced. Merryweather had, amazingly, been building fire-fighting appliances since the end of the seventeenth century. The company became fire engine makers 'by appointment to His Majesty the King' in the early nineteenth century, an accolade which enabled them to successfully develop a worldwide reputation and business. The picture shows the Chief Fire Officer and the Chairman of the Watch Committee proudly showing off their new and 'thunderous' equipment.

Right: This memorable picture of the Cammell Laird workforce streaming out of the yard in 1957, shows happy faces at having successfully completed another day of hard graft. It was not quite as simple as that, however, as unions flexed their muscles on an almost daily basis in disputes with the yard owners and with each other and life wasn't really as happy and contented as it may seem here. After the intense activity of building and repairing ships at a furious pace during World War II, the lull of uncertainty and austerity immediately the conflict was over, left a hiatus of insecurity as many families waited, sometimes in vain, for their loved ones to return home. The shipyards held on until the turn of the decade and orders began to arrive, including for the replacement Ark Royal aircraft carrier. The previous Ark Royal had been launched from the same yard in 1937 and this new order, plus several more naval contracts, provided work through the 1950s, alongside the new requirement for large oil tankers. Demarcation disputes between unions at the end of the 1950s wrecked the calm and gratitude for full employment in the yards. Sadly, a dispute as to who should chalk lines on ships' plates, between the boilermakers and the shipwrights, created industrial and economic havoc as the decade toppled, in anger, into the 1960s.

Below: The present-day Hoylake originated in the nineteenth century around the small fishing village of Hoose, as the Peninsular soaked up the demand for houses for the bosses, followed later by a demand for houses for the rest of the population. In 1830, the Mersey Docks and Harbour Board established a lifeboat station in Hoylake not least because of its strategic position on the north-west corner of the Wirral Peninsular, facing open sea. The station is one of the oldest in the country and has remained a feature of beach and sea in the town until the present. Plans are in place to provide a state-of-the-art boat for all-weather use and to cover the potential needs of several regular sea crossings to Ireland as well as increased local pleasure boating. This photograph, taken probably in the 1960s, shows the Hoylake lifeboat being moved by a tractor into the water from the beach on its trailer.

Grantreel Construction
Digging for Growth

Patrick Vesey was born in 1945 on Achill Island, in County Mayo. He was an Irish migrant worker who originally brought his experience in market gardening to the UK in 1961.

Like many Irish immigrant workers before and after he moved into the Civil Engineering industry, working on major projects such as the North Sea Gas Pipeline and the M6 Motorway, before moving onto the Wirral at Ellesmere Port, to work on the Vauxhall Plant on behalf of McAlpines.

With all this experience to fall back on, Patrick decided he wanted to work for himself and, in 1973, he bought his first machine. The company began with a contract with GCT, also in 1973, on a new development of houses, with just Patrick himself and two operatives.

Now, thirty six years later, Grantreel Construction Ltd has a workforce of approximately 90 employees across the North West of England, with 50% of them based on the Wirral. Originally, the company's offices were based

at Patrick's home in Bromborough, but, since 2003, they have been situated in new office premises at Oaklands Office Park in Hooton. Several members of Patrick's family are currently involved in the business.

The company has invested heavily in equipment, the excavator in the picture having cost £5,000 I. In fact,

the company now possesses 14 excavators valued between £45,000 and £90,000.

Through all the various highs and lows of the building industry and through the country's recessions imposing problems of minimum lending possibilities, the company has continued to invest in new machinery at every possible opportunity. The main market area for the company is working with and on behalf of the country's major house builders, including work on several projects based on the Wirral. The Parks development on Meols Drive is one of the most prestigious developments on which Grantreel has worked. Work continues on 16 developments from Preston in Lancashire down to Abergele in Wales; 5 of these developments are on the Wirral.

Grantreel has grown year on year since its inception, specialising in groundworks and civil engineering, having worked with many of the major house builders in Britain together with designing and building its own smaller developments. The company's turnover has increased from £20,000 in 1973 to roughly £9 million currently, demonstrating the reputation which has been built up over the last thirty years, due in great measure to the high level of professionalism of its hardworking staff.

*Top: Founder, Patrick Vesey. **Left:** The first machine purchased by the company in 1973. **Below:** A recent Grantreel project at Williams Lane Preston.*

James Cubbin & Sons - Making it Better for Local People

The first pharmacy in Neston was opened in 1892, by J.G. Lee, next door to the Town Hall. The business prospered, as did the family, with three of his four children joining the firm. Later, a second pharmacy was opened next to the tower on The Cross, although this closed in the 1920s. Older residents still remember the family- Miss Winifred, a local magistrate and staunch member of the parish church together with her sister, Miss Elaine, who ran the shop. Their brother Brian continued the business after it closed in 1968, by moving himself down to Bridge Street to join Harry Kenny, who had opened his pharmacy there in 1949, next to the Coach and Horses. All the prescription ledgers and formulas from Lees were faithfully transferred along with Brian who at 65, had decided that he was too young to retire!

In March 1970, James Cubbin joined the pharmacy at 7-9 Bridge Street, Neston where he was initially the manager. Jim had been

*Left: Founder, James Cubbin. **Below:** Galen Pharmacy, Bridge Street, Neston.*

apprenticed to Edward P Davies at Boots the Chemist , Leece St Liverpool in 1946. He had qualified as a Chemist and Druggist in July 1951, but since he was not yet twenty one had been too young to register.Following his National Service in the RAF, Jim returned to Boots and stayed with them until 1958 when he became a Medical representative for Messrs Woolley and Arnfield, covering North Wales, South Liverpool and the Isle of Man. Following mergers with Evans Medical and Vestric he became branch Pharmacist and Hospital Sales Manager in Speke and enjoyed the challenges of wholesaling across the whole of the North West of England..

Jim and Brian worked happily together until 1973, when Brian's decision to retire 'again' coincided with Jim' purchase of the business. Two significant changes occurred in 1984; the business moved to its present position at 17, High Street, Neston and changed its name to James Cubbin and Sons Ltd.

In 1991, the surgery in Parkgate Road applied to relocate to Mellock Lane. This was a major decision since the doctors practice had been sited in the centre of Neston for, literally, hundreds of years. Jim had bought the dispensary adjacent to the surgery from Ann Dempster in

1988 and after a series of negotiations the surgery moved to Little Neston, with a relocated pharmacy alongside it in Mellock Lane. Walking into the modern pharmacies in High Street and Mellock Lane today, there are few clues to their roots in the history of Neston and how they have reflected the changing needs of the local population.

Jim Cubbin and his wife Heather were blessed with four sons, Ian, Alistair, Stuart and Duncan, all of whom are involved to varying degrees in the successful running of the business. Two of the four boys are qualified pharmacists whilst the youngest is a business graduate, which gave some impetus to the expansion across Wirral.

The original premises, at High Street in Neston, is called Galen Pharmacy. Galen was an outstanding Greek physician, pharmacist or medicus, who practiced in Rome around the year AD 150, including personally attending the Emperor Marcus Aurelius. His work was used as the standard pharmacy textbook until the end of the 15th century. Most famously, his Theory of Disease, revolving around an imbalance of the Four Humours remained prevalent through classical and medieval times, explaining different physical and mental characteristics in the human body.

The opening of the newly built Deeside Pharmacy in Mellock Lane, in 1992, was followed by the acquisition, in 1997, of Victoria Pharmacy, at the other end of Wirral, in New Brighton. This came on the market on the retirement of one of Jim's apprentices at Boots! The business had a number of owners from

*Left: James Cubbin (second from left) with sons Ian (left), Duncan (second right) and Stuart (right). **Below and bottom:** Interior views of Galen Pharmacy.*

the 1930's onwards, but in a strange co-incidence had been the first pharmacy opened by the previously mentioned Harry Kenny. Jim always found it amusing to reflect that his career had spanned over fifty years and kept coming round in circles.

Further expansion only took place after the sad death of James Cubbin in the year 2000. Heather, who had been active in so many different spheres of Wallasey life-as a teacher, Church Secretary and volunteer worker died three years later, in 2003.

For many long-established customers, staff and professional colleagues, this did seem like the end of an

era. Jim would have been very proud to witness his sons taking the business to a wider clientele, but with the same attention to service and detail. He would have been happy to see a continuation of his policy of regularly contributing to the future of his profession by taking on pre-registration pharmacy students. These have come mainly from Liverpool John Moores University (where he and Stuart studied) and Sunderland where Ian went in 1977.

The fact that many employees who began their time with the company as Saturday staff, returned later as full-time staff, left to have families, returning again, maybe on a part-time

basis with their children then joining as Saturday staff, says volumes about the way this family business was formed in the early years and how it happily continues today.

St. Hilary's Pharmacy in Wallasey Road, Wallasey was acquired in 2005, followed, in 2006, by the purchase of the Heswall Hills Pharmacy in Brimstage Road, Heswall.

As the emphasis of the business has changed, dispensing now makes up almost 80% of activity, with retail dropping back to around 20%. Continuing strong and positive relationships with local GP surgeries, Dental practices and District Nurses have been an essential ingredient in embracing new directives and requirements.

Top left and above: *Deeside Pharmacy, Mellock Lane, Little Neston.* ***Left and below:*** *Victoria Pharmacy, Victoria Road, New Brighton.*

into high quality, non-traditional goods to augment more generic and basic stock lines, is an area constantly being monitored. Developments in IT and the NHS communications networks are an integral part of the company's plans to provide even better services, while any future expansion plans will, of course, be restricted to the Wirral Peninsular, because local people understand local needs!

Signposting is a major part of the changing role for pharmacy and the strong interaction with patients means that this is always evident in the advice offered by the pharmacists and the staff.. New medicines and new therapies, for example nicotine replacement to help people stop smoking, alcohol advice and the Minor Ailments schemes have been introduced which increasingly help patients get healthy and stay healthy.. A continuing re-defining of the role of doctor, nurse and pharmacist in all aspects of health care, treatment and prevention, will remain a major challenge for all employed by the company.

The joy for Jim Cubbin was in being able to help in easing people's problems. He was well known for going the extra mile to help his customers; his youngest son Duncan remembers, on one Christmas Day, his father going out six times to supply help and medication to his customers. The family and staff intend to maintain this strong tradition of service to the community.

Top left and above: *St Hilary's Pharmacy, Wallasey Road Wallasey.* ***Below left and below:*** *Heswall Pharmacy, Brimstage Road, Heswall.*

The company's vision for the future includes a strategy focused on the further development of customer service and the varied role in the communities it serves. A continuing review of opportunities on the retail side, including the potential introduction of and diversification

The Abbeyfield Society

A Happy and Independent Community within a Community

The history of the Abbeyfield Hoylake and West Kirby Society stretches back to 1963. However, the seeds of the Society's work in the district were sown many years before.

In 1842, a retired naval officer, Sir Richard Pulteney, made a decision to move from Denbigh and build himself a home in West Kirby. Having stayed at Redstone House on the Seafield Estate, the attraction for Sir Richard was undoubtedly the peaceful nature of the area, uncompromised by the noise and smells of any industrial activity together with the warm and tranquil nature of the western slope of Grange Hill. Sir Richard is reputed to have paid a local mason £1,000 to construct a "square structure containing several rooms and cellars": a porch and vestibule were added by later owners, the Lear brothers.

After the death of Sir Richard, changes inevitably took place. Land transfer documents from the period show the impact on Seafield House from the extension of the London and North Western Railway into West Kirby and the laying out of railway sidings which later became part of the Cheshire Lines Joint Railway. At this time, many Liverpool based businessmen began to recognise the attraction of the western area of the Wirral as a residential area unspoilt by the inevitable onslaught and ravages of the industrial revolution and its consequences. The extension of the railway into West Kirby allowed a quick and easy journey to the eastern side of the Wirral and the very regular ferry service across the Mersey into Liverpool.

Alexander Balfour, a well-known merchant, rented Seafield House for a time until two brothers, Charles and James Lear

Above: Lear House's Sun Lounge, pictured in 1930.
Below: Lear Home of Recovery, West Kirby, in 1937.

took possession of the property. The Lear brothers were the sons of a Liverpool snuff manufacturer. Charles Lear was a recognised artist and a friend and fellow student of John Millais, his paintings having been exhibited on many occasions in London and his work is recorded by the Walker Art Gallery in Liverpool. His work often included sunsets and views of wet sand and still waters, no doubt inspired by his local surroundings at Seafield House. His flamboyant appearance and dress included "a head-dress made of a folded square of blue flannel which exactly matched the colour of his eyes and hung down over his neck at the back". In contrast, James, his brother, exercised a more sober and formal approach in his appearance, wearing a monocle and an apparently constant expression of surprise upon his face! Although both brothers were relatively modest in their habits and pleasures, James was a regular smoker of cigars. The reputation of both brothers in the community was of two polite, well-mannered and considerate men, well-respected in their neighbourhood and affectionately known as 'The Cheeryble Brothers'!

The expansion of the railways and their impact on their house and grounds caused the brothers much concern. It is, therefore, interesting to note that on his death Charles was discovered to have a large proportion of his wealth invested in railway stock! They had, fortuitously, maintained screening of the property and its grounds from the intrusion of the railway line.

On their death, it was realised that neither brother had made a will, although James had begun one, in which everything, apart from a few small legacies, was left to his brother. Charles instructed his solicitor to honour his brother's requests, which included the handing over of Seafield House to a business friend of long-standing, John Elliot (later Sir John). After much debate

and consultation, he handed over the property to Trustees to be utilised as a "Convalescent Home for Women", a purpose for which it would continue to be used until 1982.

Doctor William McAfee, a member of the well-known medical family, was appointed as Chairman of the Trustees, with the remit to supervise the opening and management of the Home. The good doctor had already established the West Kirby Convalescent Home and was an elder of the local Presbyterian Church. Dr. McAfee had produced several papers on the local climate and its particular health supporting properties together with statistics he had collected appertaining to longevity and the high proportion of elderly people in the district. As a result of his undoubted influence on local health issues, Miss Giddings and Miss Douglas, employed as matrons at the Children's Convalescent Home, were transferred to the newly established Lear Home of Recovery. A plaque was unveiled in the vestibule of the Home with the following inscription; "In memory of Charles and Elizabeth Lear. This home of their sons for over 40 years is dedicated to the recovery of the sick, 1912".

On its opening in 1913, fees paid by patients were minimised through the financial support of Sir John Elliot. Over successive

Top: A 1930s view of Lear Home's Dining Room. **Above:** *Doctor William McAfee.* **Left:** *Elliot House, West Kirby, opened in 1984.*

years, extensions and improvements were implemented and, by 1946, there were twenty-seven beds together with four bed-sitting rooms for more permanent accommodation of those ladies of limited income unable to return home. In 1946 alone, between 500 and 600 women, mainly from Merseyside, were admitted, supported and discharged from the Home. The Merseyside Hospitals Council had contributed a grant towards the costs, although the 416 patients admitted under the umbrella of the Council brought in a donation of only £45! The amount of money to be raised locally was, therefore, high, with wages at £1,700 and total expenditure hovering around £3,900. The 1946 Report specifically mentions the loss of income as a result of the nationalisation of the railways due to Sir John Elliot's bequest including £2,900 of Debenture Stock in the railways! As the years went by, the financial burden of maintaining the Home's activities increased out of proportion to the various legacies, fund-raising events and occasional windfalls.

The take-over of the Lear Home of Recovery by the Abbeyfield Hoylake and West Kirby Society was a momentous event, not without a whole plethora of issues needing to be resolved. Abbeyfield operated 8 houses in the district supporting 46 residents. The Lear Home of Recovery, on the other hand, occupied a huge building with extensive grounds and substantial maintenance costs. How would Abbeyfield benefit from the amalgamation of the two organisations and how would it be able to extend the service it offered to elderly residents beyond "supportive care"? There were many problems to resolve, including the care and welfare of the existing Lear Home residents and, inevitably, negotiations would be protracted and somewhat complicated, involving, as

they did, two sets of solicitors, the Charity Commissioners, Anchor Housing Trust as well as the resolutions and deliberations of several Lear Home and Abbeyfield committees.

The Abbeyfield Hoylake and West Kirby Society began with a survey of the needs of the elderly organised by Hoylake Council of Voluntary Service in 1963. Part of the survey was carried out by a Christian organisation, the Beacon Branch of Toc H. The survey revealed the surprising presence in West Kirby of elderly people living in desperately inadequate circumstances in houses of multi-occupation. Those carrying out the survey were somewhat incensed by what they found and were determined to look into ways of relieving the issue of loneliness and neglect in old age in the district. A news item about Abbeyfield appeared in the daily papers and Mark Tully, more recently of BBC fame, but at the time, Northern Development Officer for Abbeyfield, attended a meeting in West Kirby where the 'Abbeyfield method' was explained to members of Toc H. The concept of buying a house, converting into 5-7 bed-sitting rooms, furnished by elderly residents, supervised by a resident housekeeper and taking meals together as a family, was explained as a simple and attractive opportunity to those present, largely professional and practical people. Whilst the immediate future would demand hard work, good organisation and commitment from all involved, a formal

Top left and top right: Lear House and its lovely gardens.
Above: *Paul Allen, Chief Executive Officer of the Abbeyfield Society, congratulating resident Mrs Warhurst on her 105th birthday.*

decision was made in 1963 to form the Abbeyfield Hoylake and West Kirby Society, with Mr. Hamish Craig as the first Chairman.

Recent developments in the Society's activities demonstrate Abbeyfield's commitment to current and future requirements within the local population.

In 1984, a purpose-built home, Elliot House, was opened in West Kirby, providing homes for 9 residents, together with a housekeeper's flat. In 1985 the Society purchased a house at 2 Hoyle Road, in Hoylake and in 2001, an adjacent property was purchased to enable the extension of the existing house thereby increasing the number of residents to ten, including three flats and a housekeeper's flat. Lear House was also converted to a full Care Home for 24 residents and 2007/8 a conservatory at Hoyle Road and an extension at Elliot House were completed.

Lear House gained an excellent 3-star rating from the Commission for Social Care Inspectorate in 2007 and this was renewed by the Care Quality Commission in 2009. Major refurbishment of Lear House was completed in 2009, replacing some of the roofs, and providing an extension to the existing lounge with a new balcony to make the best of the beautiful views from the home. Improved access to the Home was also completed with further developments planned for 2010.

It is an undeniable fact that the proportion of the elderly as a percentage of the overall population will rise dramatically over the next decade and that locally, the area around West Kirby and Hoylake will probably see a disproportionate rise in elderly residents. Provision of care for the elderly will become a major social problem affecting the whole community and the number of dementia sufferers needing care to a lesser or greater degree will rise significantly.

People are already putting off the decision to move out of their homes for longer and their aspirations regarding services and facilities when they do move are now much higher. Inevitably, when the decision is made, future residents will want to know

they can remain in their new home as they become frailer and that care services will be available to them. The Abbeyfield Hoylake and West Kirby Society is taking all these factors into account in developing new services and accommodation in the area.

Abbeyfield is a unique organisation in that it is run entirely by a dedicated team of volunteers, some of whom act as Trustees for the Society. The Society itself is affiliated to the Abbeyfield Society which is a national charity supporting over 7500 residents in nursing homes, care homes, and sheltered housing throughout the United Kingdom.

The Abbeyfield Hoylake & West Kirby Society will continue to strive to provide services which meet the developing needs of the elderly in this area, supported by a team of dedicated staff providing the highest standards of care and support to 44 residents. More information is available from their website www.abbeyfieldwestkirby.co.uk

Above left and Above: Garden parties for residents and their families. Below: The Abbeyfield Society's dedicated team of volunteers.

Gordale Nurseries - Planting the Seeds for a Green Future

Today, gardening remains as it always has been as one of Britain's most popular spare time activities attracting a wide range of followers, both experts and beginners. On the Wirral Peninsular, alongside the Chester High Road at Burton, Gordale Nurseries has been serving gardeners from miles around for over 60 years, continuing to develop its reputation as 'Britain's Best Garden Retailer'.

had allocated them 600 acres of pioneer land. Unfortunately for them, at the time, but fortunately for us, Gordale failed to reach the auction reserve of £9,500 by £50 and the family decided to withdraw it from sale.

Harbouring hopes of a revised offer which never came, the family began to form a different view of their future. Their ideas for moving Gordale Nurseries forward coincided, fortunately, with the country's burgeoning love affair with the motor car, providing the possibility to motor 'out of town' to specialist suppliers and providers, an opportunity which had not previously been possible. In the mid 1950s, the range of products stocked had increased. A major catalyst for this was a visiting Dutch traveller, Fred de Jong, who persuaded a reluctant Harold Nicholson to stock ornamental shrubs such as Rhododendrons, Camelias, Conifers, etc, on a full sale or return basis. These plants were an immediate hit, a novelty for gardeners and all were sold. Each year more were bought and tempted by this first success Harold bought more plants every year and to this day Gordale still trades with the de Jong family making them, at more than 55 years, Gordale's longest serving supplier. Over the years more non-family were employed and the smallholding grew, buying a greater variety of goods to sell, originally from Liverpool market.

Gordale Nurseries was founded in 1848 by Harold and Joyce Nicholson and Albert and Lilian Whittaker (Joyce's father and stepmother). After moving from Padiham in 1925 Albert had run Abbey Dairies in Manor Road, Hoylake. In 1944 Joyce had married Harold, the boy next door. He was a World War 2 Mosquito Navigator and on his demob they went to Wiltshire where they ran a bull breeding programme.

In 1948, fed up of early morning milk runs, Albert decided to buy Gordale, then a small holding and invited his daughter and son in law to come and help. He paid £9500 and initially ran the business as a market garden with pigs and hens and also grew cut flowers, vegetables and salads, all of which they sold from the roadside. They also ran a café using home-grown produce, becoming famous for their chicken salads sold to ramblers, cyclists and motorists.

By the 1950s, the family had become a little frustrated and felt that to succeed in life they had little choice but to emigrate. In 1952 they obtained tickets to go to Canada, a country with great opportunities, where the government

This page's pictures: The café, 1948 and the first shop in 1950.

The business was now run by a third generation; Peter Nicholson, who began working for the company in 1977 after training in the UK and abroad. Peter was later joined by his wife Jill, who left teaching in 1989 to work full time for Gordale Nurseries. Over the years more staff were employed many of

these employees now have over 20 and some over 30 years service with the company. With staff turnover so low loyalty and commitment has always been high, with resultant benefits to the company and customers alike.

After a 20 year gap a new café was opened in 1984 when an ice cream machine was purchased. Over the years the café has developed into an extremely popular 180 seat coffee shop, selling quality home-made foods. The customer base for Gordale is predominantly with residents of the Wirral, Cheshire, North Wales and Merseyside, with some customers travelling over 50 miles to experience Gordale's reputation for a friendly and knowledgeable service. In more recent times competition has, of course, increased, mainly from non- gardening companies such as supermarkets. Gordale has risen to the challenge by adapting in many ways. Lighting, furniture, giftware, pictures and food have been added to the range of goods on sale to encourage all year round trading and the possibility of retaining the same trained staff throughout the year.

The company has a thoroughly earned reputation for selling top quality goods at good prices and for serving the local community

in particular. Their Mission Statement declares that the company intends to 'be the best at what we do in terms of giving good service'. Recent changes include greater use of IT to control stock levels more effectively and efficiently and future ambitions include increasing the retail space to further improve presentation and service. Gordale plays an important part in the local community supporting local organisations and charities, runs a Christmas Grotto and encourages school educational visits. Special events are held regularly, including Fruit, Orchid and Bonsai Festivals, Art Exhibitions together with free gardening talks and demonstrations. The success of the company can be placed firmly in the family's focused commitment in developing a sustainable market for an appropriate range of products and services around the core garden centre business. With that important combination of loyal staff and loyal customers, the company is in a position to thrive on the deep and abiding interest of the population in gardens and all things green and growing!

*Top: A view of the expanding nursery in 1969. **Above left:** Busy parking area in the 1960s. **Below:** Founder Joyce Nicholson with her daughter Janet Riley (back row), her son Peter Nicholson, Managing Director (standing) and Jill Nicholson, Company Secretary (seated).*

W.E. Parsons
Always Aiming to Exceed Expectations

The business of W.E. Parsons & Company Ltd., was founded in 1946-7 by William Eric Parsons. William had previously worked for J.W. Flather & Company, as a Civil Engineer on a variety of projects.

In setting up W.E. Parsons, William created a civil engineering contracting business, carrying out mainly road, drainage, and public realm works in Cheshire and North Wales.

Originally, the company was based for 7 years at The Old Brickworks in Lime Street, Ellesmere Port, from where it moved 52 years ago, to Victoria Road in Ellesmere Port.

During the early years of the Company, Fred Oldham was employed as the Company Secretary and was also a director of the company, eventually leaving in 1968. Jack Copple, who originally owned a plant hire business which hired machinery to W.E. Parsons, joined the company as a director in 1954 and managed all the outside contracts until his death in 1970.

In the early days, local quarries around Ellesmere Port, Chester and North Wales were accessed for sand and stone, which was transported in 10 ton wagons. For larger contracts, then and today, modern and appropriate vehicles and machinery are rented to supplement the company's own fleet.

John Copple, Jack Copple's son, had joined the company in 1957 as a trainee and in 1970 he took over the running of the company, as Managing Director. He was involved in a variety of

projects, including between 1974 and 1994, managing a massive programme of work in Runcorn New Town, building roads, car parks and working on the construction of sewage systems. At this time, the company employed a bigger workforce, but as technology and equipment improved, the company was able to operate with smaller gangs and more specialised machinery.

During this period, W.E. Parsons had added some more unusual and challenging projects to its portfolio. The ancient Roman amphitheatre in Chester was prepared by W.E. Parsons for an impending archaeological dig on the site and the company was also responsible for constructing walkways from which the public could view the progress of the dig. Contracts with British Waterways to upgrade canal tow-paths on the Shropshire Canal, as well as on stretches of canal in Stoke-on-Trent, were completed and opened up a new area of potential activity.

Variety of work, introduction of new technology and the requirement to compete as a small company, with much larger enterprises when tendering for local authority contracts, has ensured that the company constantly up-dates and modernises its equipment. Three small wagons, JCB Excavators and Mini-Diggers provide the core equipment for most of the activities today. The Mini-Diggers have revolutionised the approach to hard-to-reach sites, where previously, large gangs of site workers were needed to manually extract earth and masonry. With access to this modern technology, the business has, inevitably, become less labour intensive, enabling them to maintain 'a tight ship' with a core workforce of around 10 employees. A smaller workforce has also made it easier to successfully manage a more intensive, industry-wide emphasis on Health and Safety.

On John Copple's retirement in 2007, his son-in-law, Richard Walters, became Managing Director. Richard had joined his father-in-law in the business in 1994, from a welding background.

The company is maintaining its position in the market place despite the pressure of current financial circumstances and will look to plan a possible expansion as the country's economy picks up. Certainly the market has become smaller, with tighter budgets within local authorities and generally less spending.

The majority of contracts taken on by W.E. Parsons are with local councils. Operations have remained constant over 60 years with similar contracts completed with the same quality approach. This emphasis on quality and promptness of completion, together with the advantages of control in a smaller, local business, will, undoubtedly enable W.E. Parsons to continue to successfully tender and compete for civil engineering contracts in the area.

Top, facing page: Tow path works at Festival Park and Etruria, Handley, Stoke-on-Trent. **Bottom left, facing page:** W.E. Parsons' completed work on part of the River Dee Cycleway in Chester. **Above:** Plant in the yard at W.E. Parsons. **Below:** An aerial view of the completed public realm works at Leadworks Lane Park, Chester.

Cereal Partners UK - Following a Cereal Without End

In 1848, John Latham and Company Ltd. opened a factory in Liverpool, producing baking foodstuffs from locally produced flours. Due to the city's strategic activities in support of the war effort, Liverpool received unwanted attention from the Luftwaffe during World War II and, as a result of bomb damage and re-development at the end of the War, the company made the decision to move to new premises in the Wirral and a new factory was eventually built at Port Causeway in Bromborough and opened in 1948 manufacturing cakes and cake mixes.

Eleven years later, in 1959, the business was taken over by an American company, General Mills Industries, producers of the famous 'Betty Crocker' range of cake mixes. General Mills had bought the factory with the intention of launching their cake mixes in the UK. This was to prove unsuccessful at that time and, three years later, General Mills sold the business. They did, however, leave behind some prototype equipment for making cornflakes.

Robertson's were a jam company that was rapidly expanding at the time and saw a link between home-made cakes and jam, a link which persuaded them to buy the Bromborough factory. Subsequently they were able to expand the range of the business to make breakfast products such as 'Corn Flakes', a 'Wheat Bisk' and a muesli product.

Viota Foods Limited was taken over by Robertson's Food Group in 1962 and moved its operation to Bromborough. It had originally started as a cake-mix business in London in 1907. With its arrival at the Bromborough site, the company continued to diversify into the manufacture of breakfast cereals.

In 1981, the factory changed hands once again and was taken over by a larger cake company called Avana. During this time, breakfast cereal manufacturing continued to be developed, with considerable demand coming from supermarkets for their 'own-label' concepts.

Above: Early products manufactured by Latham & Company.
Below: The production of Corn Flakes in the 1950s.

established with plans for a new central palletisation project to come on stream in 2010.

A major development also due in 2010 is a Combined Heat and Power facility (CHP), enabling environmentally efficient generation of electricity and steam.

Currently, the factory manufactures 'Multigrain', 'Oat and Honey Cheerios' for Nestle, together with a range of 'Private label' flakes and rice products along with 'Variety Packs' for the major supermarket chains.

From its humble beginnings, the factory now covers 25 acres and currently produces approximately 68,500 tonnes of breakfast cereal per annum. Cereal Partners have invested heavily in expanding the site and installing new plant and equipment with an increasingly healthy and environmentally sound future in mind.

The Rank Hovis McDougal Company bought the Avana business in 1987, combining the Bromborough facility with the 'Shredded Wheat' factory in Welwyn Garden City, which they had acquired from Nabisco and a wheat flake manufacturer in Watford called 'Finkins'. At this point, the cake-mix business was transferred from Bromborough to a factory in Nottingham, run at the time, by Phil Ruebotham, later to become Managing Director of CPUK and the Bromborough factory dedicated itself entirely to breakfast cereal manufacture.

Cereal Partners bought the Rank Hovis McDougal cereal division in 1991. The two partners, Nestle and General Mills (which had briefly owned the site in the 1960s), complemented each other with the different skills which they each brought into the partnership. General Mills strengths were cereal technology, equipment and its range of cereal products whilst Nestle had a world-wide distribution network with strong sales and marketing departments linked to a high-profile reputation.

In 2002, wheat flake production was transferred from Finkins of Watford and in 2003, the adjacent Sabwabco site was bought and demolished for the Phoenix packing hall and warehouse extension to be established. This was opened in 2004, with a new coated flakes plant, Project Alpha installed in 2006 followed by an additional Branflake system in 2007. Further development in 2009 saw a new coated rice packing hall

This page: One wonders if while laying this foundation stone in 1948, John Latham would have ever imagined that in 2009, the same factory would cover 25 acres and produce 68,500 tonnes of breakfast cereal a year. *Below:* Apart from the name, this view of the building today has not changed from how it would have looked back in 1948.

Quinns of Greasby - The Final Service with Care

In 1956, David Quinn, the founder of Quinns of Greasby Ltd, began taxiing part-time, mainly for friends and servicemen based at West Kirby RAF camp, using a green 1952 Morris Oxford Mk 1. This part-time work subsidised his day job, working as a technologist at Hough's timber importer in Hoylake. In 1959, David met and married his wife, Julie, who also had a part-time job taxiing after her day job, working in catering at Coopers in Church Street, Liverpool.

The taxi business grew, undertaking contract work which involved driving all over the country, no mean feat in the 1960s, with awful routes and weather to contend with. The business progressed into conveying brides to their weddings, whilst the idea for carrying out funerals came after working part-time for a funeral director as bearer/driver. This extra dimension to the business would enable David and Julie to provide a better upbringing for their increasing brood.

In the beginning, staff consisted of David and Julie, but as the activities and workload increased, more staff were required to enable them to manage the extra business. It was a friendly place to work with staff and family living and working alongside each other. Originally, the business was run from Barker Lane, Greasby, where David lived with his mother but after he and Julie married, they ran the business from their new family home, in Lloyd Drive, Greasby. Finally, in 1966, they moved the company to Greasby Road, which remains the company's main branch, having recently undergone a major refurbishment. In 1977, a first satellite branch was opened at Grange Road, West Kirby, followed by premises in Market Street, Hoylake, in 1982.

All premises are situated at the heart of their communities and easily accessible to clients.

Over the years, all eight of David and Julie's children have been employed full-time in the business and today, five are still actively involved, although as shareholders, all eight are integral to the running of the company. Currently there are three generations of the family employed, David as Managing Director, five of his children and one grandchild. It is the kind of business where roles are not rigidly defined and everyone 'mucks in', as and when necessary, to keep things running smoothly.

When the company first began undertaking funerals, it wasn't feasible to purchase a fleet of vehicles, so appropriate transport was sub-hired from a local company. However, the company can now offer a choice of either traditional or modern Daimler or

Top: Founder, David Quinn and wife Julie on their wedding day. *Above:* Julie Quinn in the one of the company's early cars. *Left:* Quinns Greasby premises prior to refurbishment. *Below:* The site of Quinns Hoylake in 1982 before refurbishment.

1990s and today. Whilst the main market in funerals is still at need, with the cost of funerals having doubled over the last ten years, pre-need plans are a huge emerging market which has to be catered for to ensure future business: pre-payment plans are now much more acceptable and less taboo than they were 10 years ago. The market for satellite services and highly designed concept products has expanded over recent years, emphasising the demands of clients to be aware of all available choices, but

Mercedes vehicles. The biggest change to the profession has been the amount of choice that has become available to clients, from very personalised coffins to diamonds made from your loved one's ashes.

One of the biggest challenges, from the early days of the business onwards, was the running of the company together, as a couple, with the dedicated hours required whilst also raising a large family: sacrifices over the years included no family holidays together, the funeral profession being a 24/7 business. It wasn't as if one could simply ask somebody to mind it for a week!

Economic pressures have affected this business, as they have many others; however, in the recession of the 1990s, many of the company's bad debts created, in their wake, a huge cash flow problem. In this business, an invoice for services is raised after the funeral and with many third party items paid for upfront on a client's behalf, the problem was created.

More recently, a huge challenge personally for the family and its business, was the loss of Julie; obviously, it affected family members greatly at the time and continues to do so today. The only positive thing it has brought is the very personal empathy which the family are able to offer to clients having experienced grief and loss themselves.

World War II has had a long-reaching effect on the funeral profession for decades. Under normal life-expectancy, those who died during the war would not have died until the 1970s, 1980s,

without any pressure selling. Today, clients are aware of their rights as consumers, even in bereavement, ensuring that, rightly, they demand the best possible service.

The future will require continuing investment in education for staff, along with an effective and seamless succession for the Managing Director, offering the opportunity to fully integrate new and fresh ideas. Quinns of Greasby, as an independent and family run business, will continue to offer the best possible, professional service, with a philosophy that nothing is too much trouble for clients and with the aim of making bereavement more manageable.

Above, both pictures: *Mr Quinn welcomes the Mayor and his wife to celebrate Quinns' 50 year anniversary and the opening of the newly refurbished Greasby branch (above).* ***Below left:*** *Mr Quinn making sure proceedings go without a hitch on a horse drawn funeral.* ***Below:*** *Some of the team outside the main branch in Greasby.*

Carmet Tugs - Ebb and Flow, Tug and Tow!

term contracts on a range of major projects, acting on behalf of dredging and civil engineering companies.

With a versatile range of tugs and other vessels and through a contract providing all towage operations on the Manchester Ship Canal since 1989, the company has demonstrated its ability to successfully manage all the requirements of harbour towing. An additional contract for manning the locks at Eastham was added to the company's portfolio in 1993.

Top left: Tugs 'Viceroy' and 'Volant' assisting Polish tanker' Professor K. Bodanancz', off Runcorn lay by on the Manchester Ship Canal, after discharging molten sulphur. Below: Tanker 'Pyla', leaving Eastham Lock under tow and bound for Shell Stanlow. Bottom, left and right: Tug 'Audrey', loading empty barges into 'Baco Liner 3' at Seaforth Dock, Liverpool. These barges carry 800 tons of Cocoa Beans from West Africa.

The Carmet Tug Company was founded in 1971 by Captain Ian Metcalfe, the present Managing Director and the late Captain Michael Carrier. Originally, towage around the coast of the UK and near Continent, plus offshore civil engineering projects were the company's main objectives.

Over the last thirty eight years, the company has successfully carried out tows of all types of floating plant, from floating cranes, dredgers and hopper barges plus a wide range of civil engineering equipment, all safely delivered to destinations across Britain and Europe.

Contract towing of disabled vessels in all weather conditions from the Western Approaches and the Irish Sea has been successfully achieved with safe delivery to ports of refuge. The company has carried out longer-

In the early 1990s, the company was also responsible for the towage of new build hulls from the Black Sea for fitting out in Europe.

In the 1990s, film and TV industry contracting was added to the company's portfolio, with film extras and boats provided for films such as '51st State' and 'First Knight' plus TV advertising and programmes such as 'Country File'.

and moved on in 1965 to the Port of Preston. In 1967, Mersey Docks and Harbour Company commenced building Seaforth Container Terminal and required large amounts of stone. As a consequence the civil engineering contractor John Howard appointed Ian as Marine Superintendent to transport the stone in barges from Dinmore, North Wales.

Top left: Tugs 'Victory' and 'Viking', towing tanker 'Mostraum' from Stanlow Refinery to Eastham Locks. *Left:* Tug 'Audrey' and launch 'Venom' towing survey vessel 'Chartwell' from Bromborough Slip to Birkenhead Docks. *Top right:* Captain Ian Metcalfe, Managing Director and founder of Carmet Tug Company Ltd. (left), with John Craven on board the launch 'Venom', on the Ship Canal during the making of the BBC's 'Countryfile' programme. *Below:* The company's Manchester Ship Canal Tug Fleet at their berth in Eastham Sluiceway.

The company has supplied vessels, from wooden boats to modern vessels, including vessels for use as film platforms and has also worked with the Central Office of Information in the production of sea safety documentaries.

Ian R Metcalfe, a founder of the company, is an old boy of Wallasey Grammar School and commenced his sea-going career with Canadian Pacific on the North Atlantic passenger run. He became Tug Master with Furness Withy in 1959

Mostyn House School
Doing Their Duty & Liking It!

The origins of Mostyn House School can be found in the junior department of Tarvin Hall School, situated in the village of Tarvin, 5 miles east of Chester. This department was established in 1854 as Lower Hall, in a building in Tarvin High Street, opposite the church. John Brindley, who ran Tarvin Hall School, appointed a young clergyman, the Reverend E.H. Price, to run the Lower Hall. Before taking up this post, we should note that Edward Price was already married to his housemaster's younger sister and thus became the brother in law of the Reverend Algernon Grenfell.

In 1854, Price made the decision to take full responsibility for the running of the Lower Hall and found premises in a former hotel in Parkgate, 16 miles away. Price leased the hotel and re-opened his school there in 1855. By 1861, the Prices had eight children of their own and a move to larger premises became urgent.

Price invited his wife's nephew, A.S. Grenfell, to take over the school, an offer which he accepted. A.S. Grenfell was the son of the Reverend Algernon Grenfell, Price's brother-in-law; having attended Rugby and Balliol College, Oxford, ASG, as he was known, had taught at Repton before accepting Price's invitation to take over at Parkgate. Arriving in Parkgate, he found things

not as described by Price and, by 1875, had set about improving conditions at the school.

ASG was headmaster from 1863 to 1882 and, importantly, the first of a dynasty of Grenfells to be involved in the running of the school. After six years of the headship of the Reverend W.F. Barrett, Algernon George Grenfell, the eldest son of ASG, rebellious and restless as a student, reluctantly took on the lease of Mostyn House, serving as headmaster from 1890 to 1933. Persuading his family to

alter his father's trust fund so that he could own Mostyn House outright, he began a programme of rebuilding, extending the school by trebling the floor space. The completion of the chapel in 1897 symbolised for AGG the progress of the school, from 18 pupils at the beginning of his tenure to becoming one of the largest schools of its type in the country, with 103 pupils. A range of new buildings and refurbishments were completed in the 1890s and, whilst the whole school had been refurbished and brought up to date, its origins were still apparent.

Mostyn House was a preparatory school which prepared boys aged 8 to 13 for entry to public schools, yet AGG only belatedly joined the Association of Headmasters of Preparatory Schools in 1899 and, although elected to its committee in 1906, was not active in its affairs. A success for this organisation was the introduction, in 1904, of a Common Entrance examination, to be sat by preparatory school pupils wishing to move on to public schools.

AGG was also an inspiration to the Parkgate community, building houses and public swimming

*Top left: Founder, the Reverend E.H. Price. **Left, both pictures and below:** Views of Mostyn House School in 1894 (top), 1905 (centre) and the new Parade front in 1933 (below). **Top:** A.S. Grenfell, headmaster 1863-82. **Above right:** A. G. Grenfell, headmaster 1890-1933, pictured with his dog Rags.*

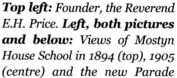

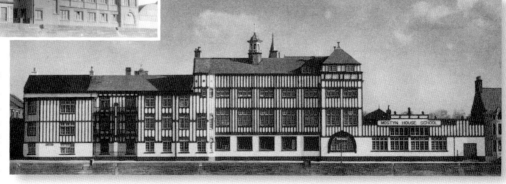

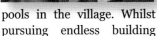

pools in the village. Whilst pursuing endless building projects with energy and enthusiasm, AGG was also a pioneer of the written word. He produced a school magazine, 'The Griffin', from 1893 to 1900, the Grenfell Spelling Book, wrote numerous hymns, a version of the Psalms and a book of rules for every pupil called 'Loyal Devoir'. This book demonstrated a positive and pro-active approach to discipline, with rules carefully explained in detail. By interpreting the school motto, 'Loyal Devoir', as 'Do your duty and like it!', he demonstrated a depth of humanity and understanding. AGG discovered a type of handwriting called sloping script in 1918, ensuring that every boy would learn it and this sloping script remained part of the Mostyn House education system until 1959.

AGG proved a dynamic and relentlessly creative headmaster, who drove the school forward over 40 years, ensuring that it embraced new and modern ideas. His son, Daryl, joined the staff in 1927 and became headmaster on AGG's retirement in 1933. Being less academic and more practical than his father, his role was more as manager than teacher. Pupil numbers increased to 150 by 1945 and AMD saw the school through the difficult war years, sustained still by the enduring vision of his father's time.

Daryl died in 1964, and was succeeded by his son, Julian, who, whilst inheriting his father's practical side also possessed AGG's willingness to listen to others and their ideas. He reformed the curriculum, re-instating subjects which AMD had discontinued as not necessary for passing of exams. Science became a major subject at the school with a new laboratory built.

In 1975, the school became co-educational, in 1979/1980 a new swimming pool was built and from 1985 the school no longer admitted boarders, but accepted older pupils and created Junior and Senior departments. As part of the transformation and with 300 pupils, a computer room, a

design and technology department and new art and music departments were created. Julian's sister, Jane Macdonald, had run Brynhir School for young children for 38 years before retirement in 1992. Mostyn House, at this point created an Infant department, and Brynhir House became a nursery for babies and pre-school children.

Julian retired in 2002 after 38 years as headmaster and his successor was his daughter, Suzanna Grenfell, who, after attending Mostyn House, was educated at Howells and Stowe, completing her studies at Wadham College, Oxford.

The changes which have occurred at Mostyn House over the last 150 years, and under six generations of tenure of the Grenfell family, have been dynamic, visionary and with an eye for exploring new directions, possibly explaining its success in satisfying the educational needs of its pupils and their families.

*Top left, both pictures: A.M.D Grenfell (left), headmaster 1933-64 and A.D.J. Grenfell, headmaster 1964-2002. **Above left:** The school crest and motto, 'Loyal Devoir', translates as 'Do your duty and like it!' **Above:** A modern montage of Mostyn House pupils. **Left:** Suzanna Grenfell, headmistress 2002-present. **Below:** Mostyn House School, 2009.*

Bromborough Paints - A Colourful Contribution

The business of Bromborough Paints was founded in 1948 by Harry Wellings. Harry had begun his working life at the local Planters margarine factory, assuming at the time that this would be the start of a great career. Unfortunately, when inexperience led to a bit of carelessness on his part the company had 'other plans' for Harry and some months later he found himself apprenticed as a joiner on a nearby housing development, successfully followed by continuous work on a succession of further developments. As the interrupted start to his working life became a distant memory, life for Harry took a turn for the better when he met Grace, to whom he was married for over 60 years.

The onset of World War II in 1939 saw Harry, as a builder, in a designated 'reserve occupation'. Initially, he found himself using his joinery skills at Hooton airfield to repair wood-framed Avro Anson aeroplanes before being sent to Birkenhead to repair homes damaged in air raids. Here, Harry met Bill McDermott and Alf Norman and together they set up NMW, continuing to work on war-damaged property. Called up as a vehicle fitter with the RASC, Harry found himself in France after the D-Day landings and involved in the Battle of the Bulge.

On a visit back to Liverpool, whilst still in the army, Harry enrolled at night school and purchased a plot of land in Greenfields Avenue and negotiated his early release from the RASC. This was where the company really began, and in 1946 he resumed his partnership with Bill McDermott. They purchased a shop with a plot of land at 38, Village Road, Bromborough, and from here the business was built up. Contracts started to come in and after starting to sell mortar, sand and lime they purchased their own lime pits and mortar mills at Eastham.

Neville, Harry's son, joined the company in 1969, seven years after Bill had left the company, and is currently Managing Director. Harry's eldest son, Fred, is a stockbroker and financial analyst and retains an interest in the company as a Director. Before leaving the company, Bill introduced Harry to Bromborough Golf Club, for which Harry would be extremely grateful over his later years, captaining not only the club but also the Liverpool Society of Golf Captains.

The changes in terms of company ownership within the paint trade have often made negotiations tricky for Neville, as Managing Director of the company. Over the years, the nature of the business has changed whilst maintaining its role as a truly independent paint and wall-coverings distributor. By a conservative approach to expansion through its history, the company has developed its interests and maintained its reputation as a successful family business during three generations. In 2008, the builder's merchants business was sold to focus on the expansion of new branches opened in Chester, Northwich and Lancaster. From its original staff of two, the company now employs 120 people in 10 branches, a true mark of its ongoing success, achievement and integrity.

*Top: Founder, Harry Wellings. **Left**: Where it all began, 38 Bromborough Village Road, Bromborough. **Above**: A bird's eye view of Bromborough Paints Ltd's 38 Bromborough Village Road premises, 2009.*

Lees Solicitors LLP - Ensuring a First Rate Legal Service

Helping people buy a house, making a will, forming a business partnership, dealing with the consequences of road accidents and divorces are just a selection from the circumstances in which we may find ourselves in need of some legal advice. Sooner or later, we could all do with the assistance of a lawyer! One firm of solicitors which has been providing such advice for longer than most is that of Lees Solicitors LLP, with offices in Hamilton Square, Birkenhead, Telegraph Road, Heswall, and Grange Road, West Kirby. For over 100 years, the 'Lees Approach' has demonstrated a genuine and personal interest in helping clients to resolve their problems; today, as a result of this approach, the grandchildren and, even the great grandchildren of the founder's clients still utilise the company's services.

The company was founded in 1889 by George Frederick Lees, who had trained at Reinhart Halsall Solicitors. As soon as he was qualified, G.F. Lees set up his own office on the first floor of 45 Hamilton Square in Birkenhead, with just one member of staff; his secretary. It is certain that he could not have imagined that by the 21st century the firm which he had created would have 13 partners (principals) and employ over 100 staff in total.

The firm expanded into 44 Hamilton Square and later would occupy part of numbers 42 and 43, as well as expanding with offices in Heswall and West Kirby and generations of the Lees family followed in George Frederick's footsteps, the last family member to work for the company being Peter Lees from 1968 until his retirement in 2003.

In 1983, G.F. Lees & Son merged with F.S. Moore & Price to become Lees, Moore and Price, incorporating in 1988, Whitley & Company and Edward Lloyd & Company to become Lees Lloyd Whitley. Six years later this large group de-merged returning to its roots as Lees and Partners and, in 2007, the firm transferred to LLP status with a further re-branding to Lees Solicitors LLP.

Currently, the firm provides a wide range of legal services to businesses and individuals. The firm assists businesses with a range of corporate commercial matters including property, dispute resolution and employment law, whilst for individuals, the firm assists with divorce, wills, trusts and estates, residential conveyancing and accident and personal injury. The firm also has two niche areas of specialisation; Court of Protection, assisting individuals who lack capacity to manage their financial affairs and, Clinical Negligence, where individuals have suffered avoidable harm, injury or loss as a result of sub-standard clinical treatment.

The vast majority of the firm's activity comes from existing clients and their recommendations to others as well as referrals from other professionals. The practice holds the Investors in People and Lexcel kite marks, the latter being the Law Society's standard for practice excellence and has increased its staff by 20% over the past three years. The majority of Lees' staff are based on the Wirral and it is their strong roots in this community which provide the firm with an unrivalled knowledge of the local market place, ensuring a top quality service to local clients

whilst building upon its successes and reputation to attract new clients from all over the north-west and further afield: George Frederick would certainly have approved!

*Top: George Frederick Lees, founder of the firm. **Left:** 44/45 Hamilton Square. **Above:** Ian MacGregor, Managing Principal of Lees Solicitors LLP.*

ACKNOWLEDGMENTS

The publishers would like to sincerely thank a number of individuals and organisations for their help and contribution to this publication.
This book would have been almost impossible without the kind co-operation of the following:

Birkenhead Central Library Reference Department

Pauline Black and colleagues at Birkenhead Central Library Reference Department

Liverpool Central Library Reference Department

National Monuments Record (NMR), the public archive of English Heritage.
For further information about these images please telephone: 01793 414600
or email: nmrinfo@english-heritage.org.uk